LEO

WITCH

♌

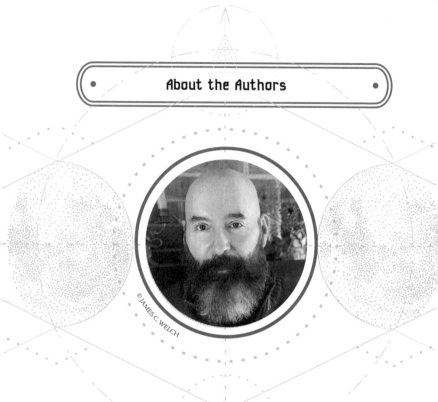

©JAMES C. WELCH

Ivo Dominguez, Jr. (Georgetown, DE) has been active in the magickal community since 1978. He is one of the founders of Keepers of the Holly Chalice, the first Assembly of the Sacred Wheel coven. He currently serves as one of the Elders in the Assembly. Ivo is the author of several books, including *The Four Elements of the Wise* and *Practical Astrology for Witches and Pagans*. In his mundane life, he has been a computer programmer, the executive director of an AIDS/HIV service organization, a bookstore owner, and many other things. Visit him at www.ivodominguezjr.com.

© SYLVIA AKENS

Coby Michael is an occult herbalist and magickal practitioner specializing in the ritual use of poisonous and psychoactive plants. He studied religion at Arizona State University and has been a folk herbalist since a young age. He owns and operates The Poisoner's Apothecary, an online shop and educational resource for The Poison Path. Coby has been blogging since 2016 for *Patheos Pagan* and *The House of Twigs* and has written articles for *This Witch Magazine* (2020) and *The Witches' Almanac* (2022). His first book, *The Poison Path Herbal*, came out in 2021. He currently resides in St. Petersburg, Florida, and travels the country, teaching people about poisonous plants. Visit him at www .thepoisonersapothecary.com/.

UNLOCK THE MAGIC OF YOUR SUN SIGN

LEO
WITCH

♌

IVO DOMINGUEZ, JR.
COBY MICHAEL

Llewellyn Publications
Woodbury, Minnesota

FIRST EDITION
First Printing, 2023

Art direction and cover design by Shira Atakpu
Book design by Christine Ha
Interior art by the Llewellyn Art Department
Tarot Original 1909 Deck © 2021 with art created by Pamela Colman Smith and Arthur Edward Waite. Used with permission of LoScarabeo.
The Leo Correspondences appendix is excerpted with permission from *Llewellyn's Complete Book of Correspondences: A Comprehensive & Cross-Referenced Resource for Pagans & Wiccans* © 2013 by Sandra Kynes.

Photography is used for illustrative purposes only. The persons depicted may not endorse or represent the book's subject.

Llewellyn Publications is a registered trademark of Llewellyn Worldwide Ltd.

Library of Congress Cataloging-in-Publication Data (Pending)
ISBN: 978-0-7387-7284-4

Llewellyn Worldwide Ltd. does not participate in, endorse, or have any authority or responsibility concerning private business transactions between our authors and the public.

All mail addressed to the author is forwarded but the publisher cannot, unless specifically instructed by the author, give out an address or phone number.

Any internet references contained in this work are current at publication time, but the publisher cannot guarantee that a specific location will continue to be maintained. Please refer to the publisher's website for links to authors' websites and other sources.

Llewellyn Publications
A Division of Llewellyn Worldwide Ltd.
2143 Wooddale Drive
Woodbury, MN 55125-2989
www.llewellyn.com
Printed in the United States of America

Other Books by Ivo Dominguez, Jr.

The Four Elements of the Wise
Keys to Perception: A Practical Guide to Psychic Development
Practical Astrology for Witches and Pagans
Casting Sacred Space
Spirit Speak

Other Books by Coby Michael

The Poison Path Herbal:
Baneful Herbs, Medicinal Nightshades and Ritual Entheogens

Other Books in The Witch's Sun Sign Series

Aries Witch
Taurus Witch
Gemini Witch
Cancer Witch
Virgo Witch
Libra Witch
Scorpio Witch
Sagittarius Witch
Capricorn Witch
Aquarius Witch
Pisces Witch

CONTENTS

✳ Contents ✳

SPELLS, RECIPES, AND PRACTICES

INTRODUCTION

Ivo Dominguez, Jr.

This is the fifth book in the Witch's Sun Sign series. There are twelve volumes in this series with a book for every Sun sign, but with a special focus on witchcraft. This series explores and honors the gifts, perspectives, and joys of being a witch through the perspective of their Sun sign. Each book has information on how your sign affects your magick and life experiences with insights provided by witches of your Sun sign, as well as spells, rituals, and practices to enrich your witchcraft. This series is geared toward helping witches grow, develop, and integrate the power of their Sun sign into all their practices. Each book in the series has ten writers, so there are many takes on the meaning of being a witch of a particular sign. All the books in the Witch's Sun Sign series are a sampler of possibilities, with pieces that are deep, fun, practical, healing, instructive, revealing, and authentic.

Welcome to the Leo Witch

I'm Ivo Dominguez, Jr., and I've been a witch and an astrologer for over forty years. In this book, and in the whole series, I've written the chapters focused on astrological information and collaborated with the other writers. For the sake of transparency, I am a Sagittarius, and the majority of the other writers for this book are Leos.[1] The chapters focused on the lived experience of being a Leo witch were written by my coauthor, Coby Michael—a scholar, herbalist, spellcaster, and maker of magickal objects and materials. The spells and shorter pieces written for this book come from a diverse group of strong Leo witches. Their practices will give you a deeper understanding of yourself as a Leo and as a witch. With the information, insights, and methods offered here, your Leo nature and your witchcraft will be better united. The work of becoming fully yourself entails finding, refining, and merging all the parts that make your life and identity. This all sounds very serious, but the content of this book will run from lighthearted to profound to do justice to the topic. Moreover, this book has practical suggestions on using the power of your Sun sign to improve your craft as a witch. There are many books on Leo or astrology or witchcraft; this book is about wholeheartedly being a Leo witch.

---

1. The exceptions are Dawn Aurora Hunt, who contributes a recipe for each sign in the series, and Sandra Kynes, whose correspondences are listed in the appendix.

There is a vast amount of material available in books, blogs, memes, and videos targeted at Leo. The content presented in these ranges from serious to snarky, and a fair amount of it is less than accurate or useful. After reading this book, you will be better equipped to tell which of these you can take to heart and use, and which are fine for a laugh but not much more. There is a good chance that you will be flipping back to reread some chapters to get a better understanding of some of the points being made. This book is meant to be read more than once, and some parts of it may become reference material that you will use for years. Consider keeping a folder, digital or paper, for your notes and ideas on being a Leo witch.

What You Will Need

Knowing your Sun sign is enough to get quite a bit out of this book. However, to use all the material in this book, you will need your birth chart to verify your Moon sign and rising sign. In addition to your birth date, you will need the location and the time of your birth as exactly as possible. If you don't know your birth time, try to get a copy of your birth certificate (though not all birth certificates list times). If it is reasonable and you feel comfortable, you can ask family members for information. They may remember an exact time, but even narrowing it down to a range of hours will be useful.

There is a solution to not having your exact birth time. Since it takes moments to create birth charts using software, you can run birth charts that are thirty minutes apart over the span of hours that contain your possible birth times. By reading the chapters that describe the characteristics of Moon signs and rising signs, you can reduce the pile of possible charts to a few contenders. Read the descriptions and find the chart whose combination of Moon sign and rising sign rings true to you.

There are more refined techniques a professional astrologer can use to get closer to a chart that is more accurate. However, knowing your Sun sign, Moon sign, and rising is all you need for this book. There are numerous websites that offer free basic birth charts you can view online. For a fee, more detailed charts are available on these sites.

You may want to have an astrological wall calendar or an astrological day planner to keep track of the sign and phase of the Moon. You will want to keep track of what your ruling

planet, the Moon, is doing. Over time as your knowledge grows, you'll probably start looking at where all the planets are, what aspects they are making, and when they are retrograde or direct. You could do this all on an app or a website, but it is often easier to flip through a calendar or planner to see what is going on. Flipping forward and back through the weeks and months ahead can give you a better sense of how to prepare for upcoming celestial influences. Moreover, the calendars and planner contain basic background information about astrology and are a great start for studying astrology.

You're a Leo and So Much More

Every person is unique, complex, and a mixture of traits that can clash, complement, compete, or collaborate with each other. This book focuses on your Leo Sun sign and provides starting points for understanding your Moon sign and rising sign. It cannot answer all your questions or be a perfect fit because of all the other parts that make you an individual. However, you will find more than enough to enrich and deepen your witchcraft as a Leo. There will also be descriptions that you won't agree with or that you think do not portray you. In some instances, you will be correct, and in other cases, you may come around to acknowledging that the information does apply to you. Astrology can be used for magick, divination, personal development, and more. No matter what the purpose, your understanding of astrology will change over time as your life unfolds and your experience and self-knowledge broaden. You will probably return to this book several times as you find opportunities to use more of the insights and methods.

This may seem like strange advice to find in a book for the Leo witch, but remember that you are more than a Leo witch. In the process of claiming the identity of being a witch, it is common to want to have a clear and firm definition of who you are. Sometimes this means overidentifying with a category, such as water witch, herb witch, crystal witch, kitchen witch, and so on. It is useful to become aware of the affinities you have so long as you do not limit and bind yourself to being less than you are. The best use for this book is to uncover all the parts of you that are Leo so you can integrate them well. The finest witches I know have well-developed specialties, but also are well rounded in their knowledge and practices.

Onward!

With all that said, the Sun is the starting point for your power and your journey as a witch. The first chapter is about the profound influence of your Sun sign, so don't skip through the table of contents; please start at the beginning. After that, Coby will dive into magick and practices that come naturally to Leo witches. I'll be walking you through the benefits of picking the right times, places, and things to energize your Leo magick. Coby will also share a couple of real-life personal stories on their ups and downs, as well as advice on the best ways to protect yourself spiritually and to set good boundaries when you really need to. I'll introduce you to how your Moon sign and your rising sign shape your witchcraft. Coby offers great stories about how his Leo nature comes forward in his life as a witch, and then gives suggestions on self-care and self-awareness. I'll share a full ritual with you to call on the spirit of your sign. Lastly, Coby offers their wisdom on how to become a better Leo witch. Throughout the whole book, you'll find tables of correspondences, spells, recipes, techniques, and other treasures to add to your practices.

HOW YOUR SUN POWERS YOUR MAGICK

Ivo Dominguez, Jr.

The first bit of astrology people generally learn is their Sun sign. Some enthusiastically embrace the meaning of their Sun sign and apply it to everything in their life. They feel their Sun is shining and all is well in the world. Then at some point they'll encounter someone who will, with a bit of disdain, enlighten them on the limits of Sun sign astrology. They feel their Sun isn't enough, and they scramble to catch up. What comes next is usually the discovery that they have a Moon sign, a rising sign, and all the rest of the planets in an assortment of signs. Making sense of all this additional information is daunting as it requires quite a bit of learning and/or an astrologer to guide you through the process. Wherever you are on this journey into the world of astrology, at some point you will circle back around and rediscover that the Sun is still in the center.

The Sun in your birth chart shows where life and spirit came into the world to form you. It is the keeper of your spark of spirit and the wellspring of your power. Your Sun is in Leo, so that is the flavor, the color, the type of energy that is at your core. You are your whole birth chart, but it is your Leo Sun that provides the vital force that moves throughout all parts of your life. When you work in harmony and alignment with your Sun, you have access to more life and the capacity to live it better. This is true for all people, but this advice takes on a special meaning for those who are witches. The root of a witch's magick power is revealed by their Sun sign. You can draw on many kinds of energy, but the type of energy that you attract with greatest ease is Leo. The more awareness and intention you apply to connecting with and acting as a conduit for that Leo Sun, the more effective you will be as a witch.

The more you learn about the meaning of a Leo Sun, the easier it will be to find ways to make that connection. To be effective in magick, divination, and other categories of workings, it is vital that you understand yourself—your motivations, drives, attractions—so you can refine your intentions, questions, and desired outcomes. Understanding your Sun sign is an important step in that process. One of the goals shared by both witchcraft and astrology is to affirm and to integrate the totality of your nature to live your best life. The glyph for the Sun in astrology is a dot with a circle around it. Your Leo Sun is the dot and the circle, your center, and your circumference. It is your beginning and your journey. It is also the core of your personal Wheel of the Year, the seasons of your life that repeat, have resonances, but are never the same.

How Leo Are You?

The Sun is the hub around which the planets circle. Its gravity pulls the planets to keep them in their courses and bends space-time to create the place we call our solar system. The Sun in your birth chart tugs on every other part of your chart in a similar way. Everything is both bound and free, affected but seeking its own direction. When people encounter descriptions of Leo traits, they will often begin to make a list of which things apply to them and which don't. Some will say that they are the epitome of Leo traits, others will claim that they are barely Leo, and many will be somewhere in between. Evaluating how closely or not you align with the traditional characteristics of a Leo is not a particularly useful approach to understanding your sign. If you are a Leo, you have all the Leo traits somewhere within you. What varies from person to person is the expression of those traits. Some traits express fully in a classic form, others are blocked from expressing or are modified, and sometimes there is a reaction to behave as the opposite of what is expected. As a Leo, and especially as a witch, you have the capacity to activate dormant traits, to shape functioning traits, and to tone down overactive traits.

The characteristics and traits of signs are tendencies, drives, and affinities. Gravity encourages a ball to roll down a hill. A plant's leaves will grow in the direction of sunlight. The warmth of a fire will draw people together on a cold night. A flavor that you enjoy will entice you to take another bite of your food. Your Leo Sun urges you to be and to act like a Leo. That said, you also have free will and volition to make other choices. Moreover, the rest of your birth chart and the ever-changing celestial influences are also shaping your options, moods, and drives. The more you become aware of the traits and behaviors that come with being a Leo, the easier it will be to choose how you express them. Most people want to have the freedom to express their individuality, but for a Leo, it is essential for their well-being.

As a witch, you have additional tools to work with the Leo energy. You can choose when to access and how you shape the qualities of Leo as they come forth in your life. You can summon the energy of Leo, name the traits you desire, and manifest them. You can also banish or neutralize or ground what you don't need. You can find where your Leo energy short-circuits, where it glitches, and unblock it.

You can examine your uncomfortable feelings and your less-than-perfect behaviors to seek the shadowed places within so you can heal or integrate them. Leo is also a spirit and a current of collective consciousness that is vast in size. Leo is a group mind and archetype. Leo is not limited to humanity; it engages with plants, animals, minerals, and all the physical and nonphysical beings of the Earth and all its associated realms. As a witch, you can call upon and work with the spiritual entity that is Leo. You can live your life as a ritual. The motion of your life can be a dance to the tune and rhythm of the heavens.

The Leo Glyph

The glyph for Leo has a few variants, but they all contain curves with flamboyant curls. Some versions are all curves, and some include a small circle as well. The Leo glyph can be seen as a lion's mane,  though the implied motion makes me think of the swish of a lion's tail. I also see it as a solar flare bursting forth from the Sun or as the classic representation of the swaying rays that surround the disc of the Sun. In the pictographic code of the astrological glyphs, circles represent spirit and semicircles represent soul. Spirit is the part of you that is eternal, and soul is the part that is shaped and changed by the experiences of incarnation. The glyph for Leo is all about the semicircles, the soul. The glyph says that you are here to live this incarnation with verve, style, and purpose. Your life is your day under the Sun, and you are here to represent its fire and glory.

With the use of your imagination, you can see this glyph as a representation of how you reach out and touch the world around you. The shape of the glyph can also remind you of the arc of the Sun's journey across the sky. There is a rising, a peak, a setting, and the cycle repeats again. This glyph reminds you to enjoy the ride, enjoy the moment, to learn, and prepare for the next day. The expression of your fire and life is both changeable and perennial. The Leo glyph is the complement and obverse to the lunar focus of the Cancer glyph. Your curves and arcs of energy reach outward rather than inward. Reaching for and expressing your passion is how magick enters you and flows through your world.

By meditating on the glyph, you will develop a deeper understanding of what it is to be a Leo. You may also come up with your own personal gnosis or story about the glyph that can be a key that is uniquely yours. The glyph for Leo can be used as a sigil to call or concentrate its power. The glyph for Leo can also be used in a similar fashion to the scribing of an invoking pentacle that is used to open the gates to the elemental realms. However, instead of the elemental realms, this glyph opens the way to the realm of heart and spirit that is the source of Leo. To make this glyph work, you need to deeply ingrain the feeling of scribing this glyph.

Visually it is a simple glyph, so memorizing it is easy, but having a kinesthetic feel for it turns it into magick. Spend some time doodling the glyph on paper. Try drawing the glyph on your palm with a finger for several repetitions as that adds several layers of sensation and memory patterns.

Whenever you need access to more of your magickal energy, scribe the Leo glyph in your mind, on your hand, in the air—however you can. Then pull, channel, and feel your center fill with whatever you need. It takes very little time to open this connection using the glyph. Consider making this one of the practices you use to get ready to do divination, spell work, ritual, or just to start your day.

Leo Patterns

This is a short list of patterns, guidelines, and predilections for Leo Sun people to get you started. If you keep a book of shadows, or a journal, or files on a digital device to record your thoughts and insights on magickal work, you may wish to create your own list to expand upon these. The process of observing, summarizing, and writing down your own ideas in a list is a great way to learn about your sign.

 Each Leo is a Sun, a star from the heavens, that must learn to walk the Earth in a way that shares their light without obscuring the light of others.

 Leo can be theatrical and showy, which some may criticize, but the root of this tendency is wholesome. You want to truly be seen because that is how you know that others know you.

 When you are at your best, you become like the Sun in the sky, bringing light, life, and warmth to the people around you.

When you lead by example and by your hard work, you are the most effective at reaching your goals. How you deal with adversity is often inspirational for others.

 When you try to control situations by force of personality and raw charisma, you may have temporary success followed by unwanted consequences.

 A Leo grows when they take a chance and reveal more of themselves (their work, their hopes, etc.) to the world.

 When you lose your center, you begin to believe your hype; you focus on the superficial things, feel unnoticed, and confuse wants with needs. This is when the need to be truly seen devolves into a need for approval. This can lead to a reliance on external sources—such as other people, substances, money, or otherworldly things—as a poor substitute for your shining light.

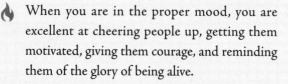

Your Leo Sun gives you more constancy and stamina to push through painful circumstances and heal from them. Even when you are heartbroken, you are good at putting on a show of strength, but make sure to tend your inner fire.

When you are in the proper mood, you are excellent at cheering people up, getting them motivated, giving them courage, and reminding them of the glory of being alive.

You are generous and caring and you love showing friends that you understand them. You try to do so in a way that demonstrates how much you know about them. This is your way of showing them that they are seen.

Just like the Sun is the hub of our solar system, you love to be at the center of things. This leads to wheeling and dealing, networking, introducing people to each other, and so on. You hold your community together and keep it going.

🔥 Dreaming big is how you prefer to approach life, and when you find that your life is shrinking in around you, it is time to dream again. There is no such thing as being too enthusiastic for a Leo, and when your emotions go flat, you need a change.

🔥 When a Leo is doing well in their life, they can spot bullies and other hurtful people and discern how to counteract the harm they cause. When a Leo is off-balance, they can become excessively prideful and melodramatic and oppress others. This weakness becomes a virtue when a Leo recognizes that risk within themselves and prevents this behavior.

🔥 There is a part of every Leo that never forgets the joy of being a child at play. This is the source of your creativity, so when you need it to come forth, let that inner Sun child come out to play.

🔥 Always remind yourself to ask for help and to delegate tasks to others. You have big dreams, and you are more likely to reach them with some help. Make sure that you express your confidence in others' skills and your appreciation for their efforts, and they will thank you for being included.

🔥 As a Leo witch, you grow in power and wisdom by finding the right balance of will, intellect, and emotion. When each of those is honored and developed equally, your inner Sun flourishes.

🔥 Regardless of your personality and preferences, it does a Leo good to be out and about in the world on a regular basis. Even if you love your solitude, unless you get opportunities to express your Leo nature, your fire may dwindle.

🔥 It's said that a person is the center of their universe, and a witch is well aware of this when practicing their craft. A Leo witch feels this deeply, and their magickal and mundane lives are improved when they bring this to mind in challenging settings. You are also your own North Star to guide you on your quest through life.

Fixed Fire

The four elements come in sets of three. The modalities known as cardinal, fixed, and mutable are three different flavors or styles of manifestation for the elements. The twelvefold pattern that is the backbone of astrology comes from the twelve combinations produced from four elements times  three modalities. As you go around the wheel of the zodiac, the order of the elements is always fire, earth, air, then water, while the modalities are always in the order of cardinal, fixed, then mutable. Each season begins in the cardinal modality, reaches its peak in the fixed modality, and transforms to the next season in the mutable modality. The cardinal modality is the energy of creation bursting forth, coming into being, and spreading throughout the world. The fixed modality is the harmonization of energy so that it becomes and remains fully itself and is preserved. Fixed does not mean static or passive; it is the work of maintaining creation. The mutable modality is the energy of flux that is flexibility, transformation, death, and rebirth.

Leo is the fifth sign in the zodiac, so it is fire of the fixed modality. This is why a Leo witch can call up power of will and passion so quickly. As a Leo witch, you can call upon fire in all its forms; it is easiest to draw upon fixed fire.

The elements and modalities on the wheel

The Sun, Your Ruling Planet

Your Sun sign determines the source and the type of energy that you have in your core. The ruling planet for a sign reveals your go-to moves and your intuitive or habitual responses for expressing that energy. Your ruling planet provides a curated set of prebuilt responses and custom-tailored stances for you to use in day-to-day life. Your Sun sign and the sign of your ruling planet are the same, and that is a gift and a challenge. There are many gods, goddesses, and other divine beings associated with the Sun. The list of attributes, characteristics, and job descriptions for these beings is lengthy and varied. Examine various pantheons and myths to see what resonates with you. I found Apollo and Ra to be useful entry points to understanding the powers of the Sun. The Sun is the source for your life force, sense of self, will, creativity, joy, and more. The Sun asks you to strive for your dreams, to be a beacon of truth and wonder, and to let go of whatever keeps you from a deep sense of dignity and poise. The Leo Sun is the fire of the heart, the hearth, and the community bonfire.

The Sun's glyph shows both that central fire and the protective circle of fire that is also your work.

Leo witches are more strongly affected by whatever the Sun is doing in the heavens. It is useful to keep track of the aspects that the Sun is making with other planets. You can get basic information on what aspects mean and when they are happening in astrological calendars and online resources. When the Sun in the heavens is in Leo, you will feel an extra boost of energy. This first step to using the power of the Sun is to pay attention to what it is doing, how you feel, and what is happening in your life. Witches can shift their relationship with the powers that influence them. Awareness makes it possible to harness those energies to purposes that you choose. Close your eyes, feel for that power, and channel it into your magick.

The Sun can be as great a source of energy for a Leo witch as the element of fire. Although there is some overlap between the qualities and capacities assigned to the Sun and fire, the differences are greater. The Sun provides the reasons why you seek something. Fire shapes how you pursue that longing. The Sun is the light and warmth that is eternal and transcendent. Fire is the light and warmth that draws from the world and is immanent. The Sun has gravitas, a pull that brings things together and creates order. Fire revels in transformation and change but is not inherently self-organizing. The Sun thwarted turns inward and diminishes or demands attention. Fire thwarted burns hotter and blazes forth into places where it should not. Over time, you can map out the overlapping regions and the differences between the Sun and fire. Using both planetary and elemental resources can give you a much broader range and more finesse.

Leo and the Zodiacal Wheel

The order of the signs in the zodiac can also be seen as a creation story where the run of the elements repeats three times. Leo is the beginning of the second third of the zodiac and is the fire that starts the second recurrence of the four elements in the story of the universe. Having come into existence, the goal of the elements at this point is to become fully established as themselves. Leo remembers their purposes for coming into being. The fire of Leo is steadfast and focused on unfolding the possibilities of existence. Although Leos are sometimes stereotyped as being too full of themselves, the deeper truth is that they know they have a mission in the world. Although true for all witches, the Leo witch needs to apply themselves to discovering who they are and where their power dwells within them. When you can consistently connect with that inner Sun that is your most authentic self, you become the power that can energize anything. You can make progress in this quest through meditation and inner journeys, but that alone will not do. The Leo witch learns by performance, by being seen, and by giving back to the world. When a Leo witch connects to the spiritual qualities of their fire, they become the sovereign of their life and create circumstances that bring joy to all.

The sign and planet rulers on the zodiac wheel

Opulence of the Sun

Lady Rhea

This spell clears out all obscurations, helps achieve honors and recognition, and brings success. The bringer of joy and a noble life, the Sun is the highest octave of all the planets and offers protection from all harm.

You will need:

+ A letter of intention
+ A mirror (approximately 8 inches)
+ A clear bowl (represents the element of water)
+ A 7-day yellow, orange, or white pullout candle in glass (represents the element of fire)
+ From any tarot deck, The Sun, Strength, and your significator (optional: no significator, choose a card that helps enhance your request—The Chariot, Ace of Pentacles, etc.)
+ 3 clear quartz or citrine crystals (represent the element of earth)
+ Incense sticks or resin (frankincense is best, but any incense you relate to is fine; represents the element of air)

Staging the Spell

Light incense to raise the atmosphere while writing the letter of intention, beginning it with "Dear Helios," or a term you resonate with for the Sun. Be explicit in your desires, being mindful of your sphere of availability. In short, ask for the best possibility, not the far-reaching cause. Sign the letter when finished, stating, "Thank you."

Beginning to Work

If needed, relight the incense now and pass your letter through the smoke. When done, place your letter where you will be working the spell. Place the mirror on top of your letter and put the bowl on top of the mirror. Prepare the candle, either leaving it plain or, optionally, blessing the top with an oil and adding herbs or glitter. Put the pullout candle in the glass holder; you can attach a photo at the top of the glass.

Add water to the bowl midway up the candle glass. Place the tarot cards on the table in a row in front of your candle spell. I like the order of Sun, significator, Strength; you may choose the combination. Place a crystal on top of each card while speaking aloud the meaning and purpose of each card. Daily repetitions of the cards' meanings are important to reaffirm the intention.

Light the candle and say the affirmation. "I, [your name], call upon the powers of the Sun to hear my call for the best outcome to my situation. [Speak your needs.] Thank you for answering my call." Leave the candle to burn as long as possible, extinguishing your candle when you are not home. Relight when home.

Incense should be offered daily along with reciting your affirmation and the purpose of the tarot cards. Change the water daily or at least every other day as stagnant water has less life force.

Seven-day glass candles may reach a point where relighting can prove difficult due to the depth of the wick. Use long matches or sticks. Dry spaghetti is another option; it will light. Tilt the candle so you can see the wick and place your implement inside. If you wish to put out your candle, simply put a lid or dish on top of the glass.

LEO
CORRESPONDENCES

♌

Power: To Will

Keyword: Courage

Roles: Executive, Artist, Politician

Ruling Planet: The Sun ♂

Element: Fixed Fire 🔥

Colors: Gold, Bright Yellow, Orange

Shape: Hexagon

Metal: Gold

Body Part Ruled: The Heart

Day of the Week: Sunday

Affirmation:
I bring the light,
but I am not the light.

WITCHCRAFT THAT COMES NATURALLY TO A LEO

Coby Michael

Ritual and spell work are performance. They are sacred theater, and we play the lead role as the witch casting the circle. We are enacting our desires and our devotion on the divine stage. Our tools are our props, guiding primal forces through the script of our intention. The spirits and deities that we call to us, and the other people involved, are all actors as well; each play an important role in the unfolding drama. Ritual performance has been part of human culture for millennia. The ancient Mystery traditions of Greece and Rome were also very performance oriented, and through the combination of group belief, ritual action, and often psychoactive plants, these ritual plays became literal happenings. These events were grand performances that turned into big parties, all with a spiritual significance—complete with plenty of sex, intoxicating plants, and sacred wine. Leos are all performers in one way or another, and we love a good party!

The performance aspect of the Craft comes very naturally to the Leo witch. I personally have found that one of my strengths is writing rituals for others to perform, whether they are grand group rites or solitary workings. I love the process of building a ritual and adding lots of nuance and panache. Our witchcraft can be as dramatic and flamboyant as we feel called to make it! This over-the-top-ness helps enhance the magickal mindset and separation from mundane life. When you become focused on ritual actions and the meaning behind them, ordinary reality falls away. The Leo witch can easily get into character, and our magickal personas take center stage. Leos are naturals at fire magick, protection spells, manifestation, love, and glamour magick; in this section, we will take a closer look at some of the ways the Leo witch is proficient.

Tapping Into Inner Fire

From my experience, witchcraft that comes naturally to the Leo witch is anything that involves the element of fire. We are fixed fire, and therefore have an innate resonance with the spirit of this element. Once it gets started, fixed fire is the most stable and long lasting, giving us the energy we need to maintain anything. The cardinal fire of Aries is like an atomic bomb, lots of energy right away, and Sagittarius's mutable fire is constantly changing. Fixed fire is contained and controlled, the gamma ray that can travel light-years. The Leo witch can connect with and channel this energy easily. By incorporating fire into our spell work, we can increase the power of our rituals immensely. Working with candles, kerosine lamps, and bonfires ignites our will and recharges our inner Sun. Fiery herbs can be incorporated in our rituals to add extra elemental power.

Protecting Passions

Protection magick comes naturally to the Leo witch. A strong and effective protection spell takes a lot of willpower to maintain, and having a personal connection to who or what you are protecting helps too. Leos have huge hearts and are great empathizers. Our spirit naturally wants to protect those in need, and we do so with a flaming sword. Fire is associated with the will, and the Leo witch has plenty. They are also proud and territorial at times, which makes defending what they love paramount as Leo is ruled by the heart. This combination of fiery willpower, protective love, and a lion's ferocity makes the Leo witch's protection spells impenetrable.

Grooming the Lion's Mane

Glamour magick or enchantment is illusion magick. It is about how we are perceived by the world around us and by those we interact with, and how we can change that perception to our benefit. It relates to what energy we are sending out into the world and the influence that it has on others. We could use a glamour spell to enhance our desirability for a job, to project success to get the upper hand in a contest, or to protect yourself when in a dangerous situation. Glamours affect the aura and the vibrations we project, but they can even be cast to bring self-confidence or to attract something desirable. By changing our auras to match what we want to attract, we put out a similar frequency (and like attracts like).

The Leo witch loves a good show and, as master of the stage, can morph into just about any character. The clothes we wear, how we style our hair, our fragrances, and our jewelry all play a role in glamour magick. I have never met another Leo who doesn't like to try on clothes, nor have I met one who would turn down an accessory. This kind of conscious adornment, imbuing our body's decorations with a desired influence or vibration, is where glamour magick becomes art. The best thing about glamour magick is that it is different for every individual!

Glamour magick is also very much about self-care. Creating ritual baths to saturate your aura with seductive energy, massaging luxurious herbal-infused oil onto your body, wearing that outfit that makes you feel like the majestic lion you are! These are all empowering ways to treat ourselves, and all glamour comes from within!

Glamour magick doesn't always have to be about being beautiful and luxurious. Sometimes we need to protect those we care about by surrounding them with the protective aura of a prowling lion, or make an object seem so undesirable that people leave it alone. Lions are just as adept at hunting and stealth as they are at being in the limelight. It all comes down to charisma and acting ability, and if we can put on a good show, even the toughest critics will buy our performance. In the end, all glamour is illusion, and it is our ability to manifest that makes the illusion a reality.

Magickal Manifestation

The Leo witch is a master manifester. There comes a time in every Leo's life when we have to be reminded that we aren't necessarily the center of the solar system. However, it is this same heliocentric (Sun-centered) view of reality that makes the Leo witch so good at manifesting. All life on Earth follows the Sun. The Sun can bring life and warmth, as well as fiery destruction. All living things feel the power and pull of the Sun. In many ways, this is how the Leo witch operates, drawing what is desirable to themselves like the Sun's gravitational pull.

Creative energy comes naturally to the Leo witch. The imagination, inspiration, and willpower to bring something new into manifestation flows through us and out of us like the rays of the Sun. Oftentimes, simply holding an intention in our minds for long enough will bring it into being, forged in the fires of our psyche. The Leo witch loves dramatic rituals with sumptuous sensory stimulation. The more over the top the better for this lion. However, this isn't typically how magick manifests for this Leo witch.

When I get into a creative state, the energy can be overwhelming if it doesn't have somewhere to flow. This usually happens when I am working on a creative project that keeps my hands busy. I begin to have flashes of visions and ideas that light up my mind like lightning. When the conscious mind is occupied and the creative mind is stimulated, psychic energy flows through us like electricity through a wire. It is during this high-functioning state that many of my new projects come to light.

Love Magick

In traditional medical astrology, Leo rules the heart. This is both the physical heart and the spiritual heart and all that is associated with it. Courage, confidence, passion, and love can all be connected to the heart, and it is through healing, strengthening, and caring for our hearts that we are able to shine this light on others. Love magick can be many different things. It isn't always about sex and seduction, nor is it the manipulative kind of love magick attributed to Scorpio (wink), but it can be.

The love magick of the Leo witch is the magick of the heart. Leos want to connect to others. The Sun cannot see its own light unless it is reflected by other planetary bodies! We want people to be happy, to share their passion, and to like us (even just a little bit). We are gift givers, helpers, and fixers because that is how our light is reflected in those around us. This comes from the desire to connect with the heart energy of others, allowing for both to shine brighter together! Not everyone has a healthy heart center, and even the heart of the Leo witch can get out of whack! The desire for this energetic exchange can sometimes appear to be narcissistic, superficial, or attention hungry.

Heart health through self-care is one of the most important regular practices for any witch, but for the Leo witch in particular. We hold all our energy in our hearts and solar plexus; creative fire, burning passion, anger, and anxiety amalgamate in our body's galactic center. If we let any of our emotions get out of control, we can burn out easily! Even something as benign as a new romantic relationship can push a Leo witch's heart into overdrive. Protecting our hearts by maintaining healthy boundaries and remembering to show ourselves as much love as we would like to receive from others is necessary. It is easy for a Leo to overdo things with someone they care about, and then find themselves feeling disappointed that the same level of exuberance wasn't reciprocated.

Heart-opening meditations, heart-healthy herbs like hawthorn berry, and green stones such as bloodstone are all great ways to reinforce the heart's energy and wellness. It is also important that we balance our fiery energy with some water-related activities. This could mean drinking more water infused with intentions of cooling and calming, eating watery foods, or spending time in (or if you're like me, *near*) the water. Ritual baths and standing out in the rain are two of my favorite ways to cool off and to remind my heart that it is safe and cared for.

The Heart of a Lion

The Leo witch is an emotional creature ruled by impulse, passion, and desire. Our big hearts are like a beacon for the emotions of others, which can be a great thing, but also detrimental to us if we remain unaware. As the center of our own universe, it is easy to forget that we are not the source of *all* we feel. We can easily pick up on the emotional energy of others, amplifying and reflecting it back into the world. This can be great if it is something like *happiness* or *celebration*, but can burn everyone involved when *jealousy* and *hatred* are amplified.

This makes the Leo witch a powerful empath, one who can easily pick up on the emotions of others. This has less to do with intuition and psychic ability, in the way that water signs are empathetic, and more to do with our hearts. The Leo witch is an empath because they feel *everything*; we feel it in our hearts and in our entire being. Leos are sensitive to their energy in their environment, often picking up an amplifying emotional energy without realizing it.

Leos are all about touch and sensation, transmitting and receiving information when we come into contact with others and when we interact with our environment. This makes us natural *psychometrists*, individuals able to pick up psychic information through the sense of touch or feeling. It is our ability to feel and to empathize that gives us our charisma, makes us such good performers, and attracts others to us. We're able to step into another person's shoes easily because we can empathize with them on such a deep level.

Channeling Creative Energy and Inspiration

When the Leo witch has something they are passionate about, when they have tapped into the *fire of inspiration*, they have infinite creative energy to draw from. In mythology, this inspiration was seen to come from the gods, leaving the person in a creative frenzy. We often see this divine madness associated with poets and bards, but it is something that is tapped into by all individuals who are using their creative powers. The Leo witch is naturally adept at channeling this intense creative energy and sustaining it for long periods of time. Other people see this energy and motivation and it inspires them to pursue their own passions with fervor.

Creative energy is magickal energy; it is the very stuff that the universe and everything in it is made from! We can work with our creative pursuits to raise and direct creative energy into other areas of our life, channeling the forces that we generate when we are creating into another area of life. It is here that artwork returns to its sacred purpose, that with every masterpiece we communicate our desires to the Divine Mind.

It is important to remember that being creative doesn't necessarily mean being artistic, and that this energy can manifest in any area of life. The Sun is associated with the arts and artisans of all kinds, and this is evident in the multi-talented solar deities. Lugh, Apollo, and Freyr are just a few examples of solar deities who are also associated with talent and the arts.

The Will of a Lion

Willpower is an essential component of magickal practice. It is the driving force behind why we do what we do, why we want what we want, and what we are willing to do to achieve it. In modern magickal practice, *the will* is associated with the element fire. It is the foundation of the *Witch's*

Pyramid. Fire is the first element of material manifestation and the spark that drives our magick. In the same way that fire can be creative and destructive, the will also manifests in higher and lower frequencies.

The will of the ego wants us to think that it is our true will. The ego wants what it wants based on pleasure and personal gratification, and there is absolutely nothing wrong with that. The problem arises when we are operating completely from a place of ego. This is when we can become impulsive and give in to excess, addiction, and narcissism. Having a strong will is great when it comes to overcoming obstacles, but it can also become our own cage, trapping us by false realities. We want to operate from the place of our *True Will*, our magickal will. This is the part of us unattached to ego, the force that drives us from one lifetime to the next.

When we can connect to our True Will, things seem to manifest spontaneously. When we are on a path that is in alignment with our true purpose, we don't need elaborate rituals to manifest what we want because we are tapped into the creative energy of the universe on a molecular level. The Leo witch operates from this place naturally. We can feel the pull of our True Will, even when we do not yet understand our purpose. It seems like we are being divinely guided and protected, and in a sense, we are, but it is through our own divine will.

Sun worship is one of the oldest and most common human spiritual tendencies. It is found in virtually every ancient culture, each one having their own deities and spirits associated with this heavenly body. The Sun is typically depicted as a masculine entity, a characteristic of our current patriarchal society. It is the creative and active force in our solar system. The gods and spirits associated with the Sun take on similar themes, which can be seen in figures like Apollo, Lugh, and even Lucifer.

These are the gods of light, virility, sexual potency. They are often associated with the arts and are multitalented. They are represented by the solar child and divine masculinity, phallic gods, and rainbow spirits. They do not have to be thought of as strictly male entities, as many of them are queer in nature. The following is a list of gods and spirits who align with these ideas.

Fabulous Deities of Light

+ Apollo
+ Ra
+ Hermes
+ Lugh
+ Adonis
+ Sunna
+ Hathor
+ Freyr
+ Azazel
+ Belenus
+ Balder
+ Narcissus
+ Archangel Michael

The Strength Card

In the Rider-Waite-Smith tarot, the Strength card is depicted as a female figure dressed in white with an infinity sign above her head, holding the open jaws of a fierce lion. She does this with a calm and confident look on her face, exerting little effort. This card is about quiet inner strength and resilience in the face of adversity, and taming our inner lion. The figure in the card has tamed the lion and is able to express the fiery passion of this animal in a positive way. The lion is tamed not through brute force but through sympathy and understanding, using influence and persuasion to quietly guide the situation. This kind of quiet strength is often underestimated, but it works in the background.

It is easy to confuse strength with control and domination, trying to force ourselves into being what we think we should be. We can get carried away with trying to control every aspect of our lives, and we try to reinforce this sense of control by trying to influence others. When we nurture our inner lion, it becomes a strong protector and ally, and it is no longer our adversary.

Leo's Enchanted Sunglasses

Coby Michael

This spell combines glamour magick and solar energy with Leo's love for making a fashion statement. It is a simple ritual that involves enchanting a pair of sunglasses with colored lenses with the energy of the sun. Choose a color that matches your intention. It could be to attract romantic energy, to create prosperity, or to change your mood. Since this is a glamour, which affects our aura, it can also influence the people around us.

You will need:

+ Sunglasses of a color that matches your intention (see color association list at the end)
+ Herbs associated with the Sun, such as calendula, St. John's wort, or sunflower
+ Stones or other objects associated with the Sun, such as citrine, sunstone, or carnelian

Instructions:

You can perform the ritual on either a Sunday or a day of the week that matches your intention/the color of your glasses. Make sure it is going to be a sunny day because you want the sunglasses to soak up the Sun's rays. Place them on an altar of solar herbs, surround them with stones associated with the Sun, or draw the planetary glyph of the Sun on your altar. As they begin to soak up the Sun's energy, you want to visualize the color energy of the sunglasses to be amplified. To bring in your desired influence, burn incense associated with your intention, or light candles that match your sunglasses.

Sit and meditate in this energy, and when you feel like it is at its maximum potential, put on the sunglasses and look at the world around you. Feel the vibration of your intention flowing through you, bathing the world in colored light. You can do this simple ritual with sunglasses of every color, and wear them when you want to become a conduit for their energy.

Here is a short list of some common concepts and ideas associated with each color. These are just a starting point, and everyone has different color associations that evoke different energies.

- *Red*—power, passion, luck, sexuality, lust, authority
- *Orange*—energy, creativity, ingenuity, manifestation
- *Yellow*—happiness, inner child, new beginnings, nonbinary
- *Green*—growth, fertility, prosperity, abundance, nature
- *Blue*—healing, communication, calm, clarity
- *Violet*—spirituality, influence, mastery, mystery
- *Pink*—love, charisma, beauty, sensitivity

MAGICAL
CORRESPONDENCES

♌

While the Leo witch has countless talents, there are certain types of spells and ways of working that are more suited to our fiery Leo energy. The following is a list of techniques, ritual accoutrements, and magickal ideas that will make your inner lion shine! These are just ideas, and you can use your own creativity when it comes to your magick, but don't be surprised if you find some of these already on your list!

Types of Spellcraft

+ Conjuring creative inspiration

+ Visual and artistic magick

+ Fire magick, hearth, and candle spells

+ Sacred drama

+ Leading rituals and group workings

+ Sex magick

Magical Tools

+ Ritual wardrobe (robes, jewelry, boas)
+ Crown and scepter
+ Mirror
+ Candles, oil lamp, and ritual fire
+ Drum
+ Wand (or dagger, depending on tradition)
+ Smoke cleansing sticks

Magical Goals and Spell Ideas

+ Confidence, courage, and charisma spells
+ Protection magick
+ Summoning strength and ferocity, raising energy
+ Manifestation of desires
+ Calling a creative muse
+ Drumming to awaken warrior energy

Ivo Dominguez, Jr.

You've probably encountered plenty of charts and lists in books and online, cataloging which things relate to your Sun sign and ruling planet. There are many gorgeously curated assortments of herbs, crystals, music playlists, fashions, sports, fictional characters, tarot cards, and more that are assigned to your Sun sign. These compilations of associations are more than a curiosity or for entertainment. Correspondences are like treasure maps to show you where to find the type and flavor of power you are seeking. Correspondences are flowcharts and diagrams that show the inner, occult relationships between subtle energies and the physical world. Although there are many purposes for lists of correspondences, there are two that are especially valuable to becoming a better Leo witch. The first is to contemplate the meaning of the correspondences, the ways in which they reveal meaningful details about your Sun sign and ruling planet, and how they connect to you. This will deepen your understanding of what it is to be a Leo witch. The second is to use these items as points of connection to access energies and essences that support your witchcraft. This will expand the number of tools and resources at your disposal for all your efforts.

Each of the sections in this chapter will introduce you to a type of correlation with suggestions on how to identify and use it. These are just starting points, and you will find many more as you explore and learn more. As you broaden your knowledge, you may find yourself a little bit confused as you find that sources disagree on the correlations. These contradictions are generally not a matter of who is in error but a matter of perspective, cultural differences, and the intended uses for the correlations. Anything that exists in the physical world can be described as a mixture of all the elements, planets, and signs. You may be a Leo, but depending on the rest of your chart, there may be strong concentrations of other signs and elements. For example, if you find that a particular herb is listed as associated with both Leo and Libra, it is because it contains both natures in abundance. In the cases of strong multiple correlations, it is important that you summon or tune in to the one you need.

Times

You always have access to your power as a Leo witch, but
there are times when the flow is stronger, readily available, or
more easily summoned. There are sophisticated astrological
methods to select dates and times that are specific to your
birth chart. Unless you want to learn quite a bit more astrology or hire someone to determine these for you, you can do
quite well with simpler methods. Let's look at the cycles
of the solar year, the lunar month, and the hours of
day-night rotation. When the Sun is in Leo, or the
Moon is in Leo, or it is early afternoon, often the
hottest part of the day, you are in the sweet spot
for tuning in to the core of your power.

Leo season is roughly July 23–August 22,
but check your astrological calendar or ephemeris
to determine when it is for a specific year in your
time zone. The amount of accessible energy is highest
when the Sun is at the same degree of Leo as it is in your
birth chart. This peak will not always be on your birth date,
but very close to it. Take advantage of Leo season for working magick and for recharging and storing up energy for the
whole year.

The Moon moves through the twelve signs every lunar
cycle and spends around two and half days in each sign.
When the Moon is in Leo, you have access to more lunar
power because the Moon in the heavens has a resonant link

to the Sun in your birth chart. At some point during its time in Leo, the Moon will be at the same degree as your Sun. For you, that will be the peak of the energy during the Moon's passage through Leo that month. While the Moon is in Leo, your psychism is stronger, as is your ability to manifest things. When the Moon is in its waning gibbous phase, in any sign, you can draw upon its power more readily because it is resonant to your sign.

From an astrological perspective, the cross-quarter day of Lughnasadh is when the Sun is at the 15th degree of Leo. Whether or not you celebrate one of the cross-quarter holidays, the peak of Leo season is its midpoint at the 15th degree, and this is a special day of power for you. You can look up when the Sun is in the 15th degree of Leo for the current or future years using online resources or an ephemeris. Leo is the fifth sign of the zodiac, and the zodiac is like a clock for the purpose of spell work. Afternoon corresponds to the fiery power of Leo. If you are detail focused, you might be wondering when afternoon is. This varies with the time of year and with your location, but if you must have a time, think of it as 2:00 p.m. to 4:00 p.m. Or you can use your intuition and feel your way to when afternoon is on any given day—think the warmest part. The powers that flow during this time are rich, creative, and filled with possibilities for you to experience. Plan on using the Leo energy of the afternoon to fuel and feed spells for learning, divination, creativity, and new growth.

The effect of these special times can be joined in any combination. For example, you can choose to do work in the afternoon when the Moon is in Leo, or when the Sun is in Leo in the afternoon, or when the Moon is in Leo during Leo season. You can combine all three as well. Each of these time groupings will have a distinctive feeling. Experiment and use your instincts to discover how to use these in your work.

Places

There are activities, professions, phenomena, and behaviors that have an affinity, a resonant connection, to Leo and its ruling planet, the Sun. These activities occur in the locations that suit or facilitate their expressions. There is magick to be claimed from those places that is earmarked for Leo or your ruling planet, the Sun. Just like your birth chart, the world around you contains the influences of all the planets and signs, but in different proportions and arrangements. You can always draw upon Leo or Sun energy, though there are times when it is more abundant depending on astrological considerations. Places and spaces have energies that accumulate and can be tapped like a battery. Places contain the physical, emotional, and spiritual environments that are created by the actions of the material objects, plants, animals, and people occupying those spaces. Some of the interactions between these things can generate or concentrate the energies and patterns that can be used by Leo witches.

If you look at traditional astrology books, you'll find places assigned to Leo and Sun such as these:

 Wherever performances take place

 Fashion events, art openings, and fancy balls

 Hot spots for nightlife and restaurants

 Fire and drum circles and sunny lush gardens

These are very clearly linked to the themes associated with Leo and Sun. With a bit of brainstorming and free-associating, you'll find many other less obvious locations and situations where you can draw upon this power. For example, social settings that allow you to hold court, posh stores, public debates, and places that are beautiful and majestic can produce a current that you can plug into. Any activity where you get to shine, the planning of an event or party, making art or being creative in other ways, or similar activities can become a source of power for a Leo witch. All implements or actions related to creative endeavors, beauty and fashion, being in leadership, having fun for the sake of fun, and so on could also be sources for energy.

While you can certainly go to places that are identified as locations where Leo and/or Sun energy is plentiful to do workings, you can find those energies in many other circumstances. Don't be limited by the idea that the places must have a formalized link to Leo. Be on the lookout for Leo or Sun themes and activities wherever you may be. Remember that people thinking, feeling, or participating in activities connected to your sign and its ruling planet are raising power. If you can identify with it as resonating with your Sun sign or ruling planet, then you can call the power and put it to use. You complete the circuit to engage the flow with your visualization, intentions, and actions.

Plants

Leo is fiery, expressive, fun loving, has swag, and its color is golden, rich, deep yellow. Sun overlaps with these, but also will, vitality, and centeredness. Herbs, resins, oils, fruits, vegetables, woods, and flowers that strongly exhibit one or more of these qualities can be called upon to support your magick. Here are a few examples:

 Sunflower because it follows the Sun and strengthens friendships.

 Cinquefoil for protection in court and when taking a stand.

 Hawthorn berries because they strengthen the heart.

59

Heliotrope strengthens devotion and amplifies intentions.

 Mistletoe because it contains the spark of the dreaming Sun of winter.

Once you understand the rationale for making these assignments, the lists of correspondences will make more sense. Another thing to consider is that each part of a plant may resonate more strongly with a different element, planet, and sign. Sunflower shows its connection with Leo and Sun through flowers that follow the Sun and its use in friendship magick. However, sunflower is also used for calling the dead, and the oil of its seed is cooling, so it has lunar properties. Which energy steps forward depends on your call and invitation. "Like calls to like" is a truism in witchcraft. When you use your Leo nature to make a call, you are answered by the Leo part of the plant.

Plant materials can take the form of incense, anointing oils, altar pieces, potions, washes, magickal implements, foods, flower arrangements, and so on. The mere presence of plant material that is linked to Leo or the Sun will be helpful to you. However, to gain the most benefit from plant energy, you need to actively engage with it. Push some of your energy into the plants and then pull on it to start the flow. Although much of the plant material you work with will be dried or preserved, it retains a connection to living members of its species. You may also want to reach out and try to commune with the spirit, the group soul, of the plants to request their assistance or guidance. This will awaken the power slumbering in the dried or preserved plant material. Spending time with living plants, whether they be houseplants, in your yard, or in a public garden, will strengthen your conversation with the green beings under Leo's eye.

Crystals and Stones

Before digging into this topic, let's clear up some of the confusion around the birthstones for the signs of the zodiac. There are many varying lists for birthstones. Also be aware that some are related to the calendar month rather than the zodiacal signs. There are traditional lists, but the most commonly available lists for birthstones were created by jewelers to sell more jewelry. Also be cautious of the word *traditional* as some jewelers refer to the older lists compiled by jewelers as "traditional." The traditional lists created by magickal practitioners also diverge from each other because of cultural differences and the availability of different stones in the times and places the lists were created. If you have already formed a strong connection to a birthstone that you discover is not really connected to the energy of your sign, keep using it. Your connection is proof of its value to you in moving, holding, and shifting energy, whether or not it is specifically attuned to Leo.

These are my preferred assignments of birthstones for the signs of the zodiac:

Aries	Bloodstone, Carnelian, Diamond
Taurus	Rose Quartz, Amber, Sapphire
Gemini	Agate, Tiger's Eyes, Citrine
Cancer	Moonstone, Pearl, Emerald
Leo	Heliodor, Peridot, Black Onyx
Virgo	Green Aventurine, Moss Agate, Zircon
Libra	Jade, Lapis Lazuli, Labradorite
Scorpio	Obsidian, Pale Beryl, Nuummite
Sagittarius	Turquoise, Blue Topaz, Iolite
Capricorn	Black Tourmaline, Howlite, Ruby

| Aquarius | Amethyst, Sugilite, Garnet |
| Pisces | Ametrine, Smoky Quartz, Aquamarine |

There are many other possibilities that work just as well, and I suggest you find what responds best for you as an individual. I've included all twelve signs in case you'd like to use the stones for your Moon sign or rising sign. Hands-on experimentation is the best approach, so I suggest visiting crystal or metaphysical shops and rock and mineral shows when possible. Here's some information on the three that I prefer for Leo:

Heliodor

Heliodor comes in many yellow hues, but the best for Leo is called golden beryl. Its name means "gift of the Sun." This gem is like a ray of sunlight that clears away doubt and self-ishness and illuminates your inner demons. It also helps center you and guard against emotional imbalances. It can be used to gain states of higher mind and connection with your divine spark. It is also a seer's stone in that it helps separate what you fear or hope for from what is actually happening so you can observe more objectively. Heliodor acts as a beacon to attract your spiritual allies.

Peridot

This green crystal contains Sun's light transformed in the power of the green kingdom of plant life. It teaches that life will always find a way to prevail. It brings cheerfulness and dispels envy and jealousy. As such, peridot is a defense against the evil eye. It also heightens creativity and knowing when and how to say what is most needed. Peridot strengthens and protects the heart chakra. It helps with releasing thoughts and emotions that no longer serve you. Removing self-sabotage is one of its best uses. It can assist in letting you feel and understand how all living beings are connected and affect each other.

Black Onyx

It may seem odd for a black stone to be listed for a Leo witch, but Leo is fixed fire. Containing and focusing the flames is a virtue of black onyx. Black onyx anchors and holds your power like a hearth, a fireplace, or a fire ring, giving a controlled center to your flames. It helps keep you focused, centered, and on task. Black onyx also makes it safer for you to handle more power without losing control. This stone cuts through mental fog or overthinking and is especially good at dealing with a sense of unworthiness or imposter syndrome. Black onyx in a gold setting is particularly good for Leos.

Intuition and spiritual guidance play a part in the making of correlations and, in the case of traditional lore, the collective experience of many generations of practitioners. There is also reasoning behind how these assignments are made, and understanding the process will help you choose well. Here are some examples of this reasoning:

 Crystals assigned to Leo are often sunny, cheerful colors or have a golden sheen to them. Gold sheen obsidian, sunstone, and orange calcite are good examples.

 Leo's metal is gold, but the pure crystalline form is rare and expensive. Pyrite, fool's gold, is mostly iron and sulphur but can contain trace amounts of gold. More importantly, pyrite looks like gold.

 Crystals whose lore and uses are related to Leo or Sun actions or topics, such as performing, eloquence in speech, courage, and creativity, are recommended as crystals for Leo.

 Crystals that are the opposite of the themes for Leo provide a counterbalance to an excessive manifestation of Leo traits. For example, malachite is useful for Leo as it brings awareness of other people's needs and emotional insight.

Crystals suggested for Aquarius, your opposite sign, are also useful to maintain your balance.

Working with Ritual Objects

Magickal tools and ritual objects are typically cleansed, consecrated, and charged to prepare them for use. In addition to following whatever procedure you may have for preparing your tools, add in a step to incorporate your energy and identity as a Leo witch. This is especially productive for magickal tools and ritual objects that are connected to fire or are used to store, direct, or focus power. By adding Leo energy and patterning into the preparation of your tools, you will find it easier to raise, move, and shape energy with them in your workings.

There are many magickal tools and ritual objects that do not have any attachment to specific elements. The core of your life force and magickal power springs from your Leo Sun. So, when you consciously join your awareness of your Leo core with the power flowing through the tools or objects, it increases their effectiveness. Develop the habit of using *Leo* as a word of power, the glyph for Leo for summoning power, and the golden colors of Leo to visualize its flow. Whether it be a pendulum, a wand, a crystal, or a chalice, your Leo energy will be quick to rise and answer your call.

A Charging Practice

When you consciously use your Leo witch energy to send power into tools, it tunes them more closely to your aura. Here's a quick method for imbuing any tool with your Leo energy.

1. Place the tool in front of you on a table or altar.
2. Take a breath in, imagining that you are breathing in golden energy, and then say "Leo" as you exhale. Repeat this three times.
3. Touch your left shoulder with the fingertips of your right hand. Then lift your fingers and trace an arc over your head with your fingers coming to rest on your right shoulder. Next, hold your hands with palms close to your ears and fingers extended. You've just formed the glyph for Leo, giving you a crown or a mane if you like.
4. Now, using a finger, trace the glyph of Leo over or on the tool you are charging.

Repeat this several times and imagine the glyph being absorbed by the tool.

5. Pick up the tool, take in a breath while imagining golden energy, and blow that charged breath over the tool.

6. Say "Blessed be!" and proceed with using the tool or putting it away.

Hopefully this charging practice will inspire you and encourage you to experiment. Develop the habit of using the name *Leo* as a word of power, the glyph for Leo for summoning power, and the sunny colors of Leo to visualize its flow. Feel free to use these spontaneously in all your workings. Whether it be a pendulum, a wand, a crystal, a chalice, a ritual robe, or anything else that catches your imagination, these simple methods can have a large impact. The Leo energy you imprint into them will be quick to rise and answer your call.

HERBAL
CORRESPONDENCES

♌

These plant materials all have a special connection to your energy as a Leo witch. There are many more, but these are a good starting point.

Herbs	
Rue	for hex breaking
Bay Laurel	for clear communication
St. John's Wort	for banishing and cleansing

Flowers

Mexican Marigold	for clear psychic visions
Chamomile	for prosperity and luck
Calendula	attracts healthy energy

Incense and Fragrances

Olibanum Oil	to call balance and strength
Amber	restores the fire within
Labdanum	brings courage and hope

CLEANSING AND SHIELDING

Coby Michael

Sovereignty over ourselves and our space is important to the Leo witch, and maintaining an energetically clean and safe environment tells the universe that this space is ours and that we won't allow any unwanted energy or spirits to be here. Having boundaries and maintaining them is an important part of bringing a sense of stability and safety to the Self. We show up for ourselves and hold our space when we practice regular cleansing and shielding.

When we engage in ritual and ceremony involving other people, whether they are present or not, we form a psychic connection to that person. When it is someone we know and feel very strongly about, this connection is even stronger. It is important to remember to disconnect and to maintain the boundaries of your own personal energy field before and after ritual. This is especially true for the Leo witch, who connects with the people in their lives on a heart and soul level. The following are some techniques that can be performed before and after ritual to maintain strong energetic boundaries.

Cleansed in the Fire

Burning incense and smoke cleansing are traditional ways of cleansing people and places from energies associated with illness, death, and the forces of chaos. The following are some different herbs and resins I chose for their fiery qualities. Burning incense and offerings is one of the most ancient forms of spiritual practice, and it was believed that burning something multiplied its power. Frankincense and benzoin are two of my favorite resins to burn to raise the vibration of a space and cleanse its energy. Frankincense is considered a masculine, solar, and fiery resin. Benzoin is much sweeter and has a golden color like crystalized sunlight. These resins can be used alone or in combination to create sacred space, enter a meditative state, and attract beneficial energies.

I personally prefer to work with sweeter smelling herbs and resins when cleansing a space. Some cleansing herbs have a bitter scent, which is why they are good at getting rid of things, but they leave the room with the feeling of being doused in disinfectant. This is why I prefer to work with sweet and rich aromas, which not only cleanse a space, but fill it with sweetness.

Rosemary is another herb that makes a great cleansing and protective ally, which can be strewn around the home, burned, or made into bundles that can be used to brush the body to remove unwanted energy. Bay leaves are also great for burning for cleansing, protection, and abundance. They have a warm and spicy aroma.

In addition to burning herbs for their cleansing and protective properties, the fire itself can also be employed to the same effect. Tending a sacred fire, offering prayers, and burning herbs as offerings can be a very healing experience; the fire brings protection to everyone nearby. The role of fire keeping is of the utmost importance in most indigenous cultures. Using the flame of a candle to carefully direct cleansing or healing energy around a person is also effective, bringing warmth and blood flow to the area. This is similar to the technique used in Traditional Chinese Medicine called moxibustion. In this technique, a cloth with some ground mugwort is held over the area needing healing while the plant material is lit on fire. The fire doesn't actually come into contact with the person's skin, but brings balance to the person's energy in that area.

Lion's Roar Shielding

This technique creates a reverberating aura of power and protection around the witch to deter enemies, protect ourselves and our surroundings, and send a clear expectation of our boundaries. Sit in meditation and connect with the spirit of the lion. See it move, feline, powerful, and deadly. The lion protects its territory ferociously and is respected by the rest of the animal kingdom. Feel this power grow within you, and as it builds, imagine a low growl emanate in the air around you, growing until it becomes a deafening roar. You can join in and actually roar if you want to, but the important thing is to picture the power in the sound waves filling the air around you. If you are trying to do this quickly for your own protection, doing the roar out loud may help or hinder your situation.

Ring of Fire

This shielding technique is similar to the last one; however, it creates a circle of protection in a more definite area. It is less spread out but much more concentrated than the Lion's Roar. The Ring of Fire is a good technique to use when stationary protection is needed, such as prior to a summoning ritual. It helps to have some actual fire to create your boundary.

You will need:
+ Four red taper candles in holders or on plates, set in a 6-foot diameter circle, one at each cardinal direction
+ About a tablespoon of a finely powdered fiery herb, such as red sandalwood, stinging nettle, wormwood, or saltpeter

Stand in the center and feel the warmth from the light of the candles. Feel the fire burning within and look to the sky to see a flaming sword descend from the heavens, casting a whirlwind of fire around you. Hold this image in your mind of your circle being encased in a pillar of spinning fire and go to each of the candles. Sprinkle a pinch of your fiery herb or saltpeter directly over the flame, keeping your hand far enough away that you don't burn yourself. Allow the herbs to fall and crackle in the heat (not so much that you put the candle out!). Say,

The flaming sword of Michael descends,
scorching the earth and destroying my enemies,
cutting away all evil with holy fire.

When you have finished with all four candles, go back to the center of the circle and visualize the ring of fire that surrounds you, feeling the hot air on your face. You now stand protected, and anytime you want to call upon this protection, visualize the sword breathing its flames around you.

This technique can also be adapted to clear the energy field by moving the fire in a sweeping motion, or to destroy or remove harmful and stagnant energies by focusing it into a specific place. The Leo witch can easily access this spiritual fire, putting it toward numerous purposes.

Children of Light

All manner of healing, shielding, and cleansing can be achieved by applying different colors of light, both in visualization and in the visible light spectrum. The light can take on any form, acting as a shield keeping out negativity, a refreshing mist bringing soothing calm, or a focused laser cutting out harmful attachments.

Light is energy and vibration; the colors that we see are all different wavelengths reflecting light back at different rates. We can direct that energy and vibration for its healing and transforming effects. By visualizing the energy field around us changing color, we can bring that vibration into our aura for its desired effects. This is a similar concept to the enchanted sunglasses idea, which could also be used to project different types of healing energy through the eyes.

One way to bring together the healing powers of sunlight with the full spectrum of the rainbow is to work with prisms. There are both natural and manmade prisms that refract sunlight, splitting it into the seven colors of the rainbow. By using the prism as a tool to direct the sunlight, it can be passed over the entire body and focused on specific areas. With this technique, we get the benefit of the entire visible light spectrum, and rainbows in general are very spiritually significant.

Hanging carved crystal and prisms in your home, office, or rearview mirror is a subtle but effective way to keep the energy of a place moving and alive. Stagnant and low vibration energy is neutralized by the light passing through the crystal prism. Quartz and glass crystals from old chandeliers work great for this, or you can buy fancy manmade crystals carved in shapes that refract the light into beautiful shapes.

The Royal Wardrobe

The clothes we wear can tell us a lot about who we are. There are so many opportunities for personal expression in the way we dress and style ourselves. The Leo witch never misses the opportunity to dress for an occasion, and we love a costume party! I personally always feel more comfortable at a costume or theme event than I do in regular clothes. So, I just started making my regular clothes into costumes. This helps ease my social anxiety and makes me more comfortable around other people.

We can empower the clothes we wear to shield us from harmful energy and unwanted attention and to reflect negativity. When we feel confident in ourselves, we shine like the Sun, and this radiance envelops us in a field of positive energy. When we feel comfortable, other people feel comfortable. Our hearts are open, and a genuine exchange can occur.

When choosing items for your magickal wardrobe, it is more about how the item makes you feel than any spell you cast on it. It could be a really edgy earring you wear in one ear, a black velvet jacket that makes you look like a badass, or a pair of shoes covered in spikes and sparkles. If you feel like you are in your ultimate form when you wear this item, then it works! You can combine multiple pieces and build a show-stopping outfit, or choose unique pieces to project a specific type of energy.

WHAT SETS A LEO OFF, AND HOW TO RECOVER

Coby Michael

It's a common idea that Leos are all about themselves, and in some ways, that is true. It's taken me a while to get here, but I can safely say I love myself. It takes a lot for some people to get to a point where they feel comfortable enough to put themselves out there. So, when others say negative things to try to take away from someone else's happiness, that really bothers me. As much as I would like it to be, it's not always about me. One of my biggest priorities as a magickal practitioner is to connect with other practitioners, and to lift one another up. We all have ways we can support each other and things we are good at. This mentality of everyone for themselves, fueled by large egos and small minds, is not conducive to growth for any of us. I try to help people however I can, especially if someone is asking for it. I want to be there for people and feel like people need me. I think everyone wants to feel that way.

So, it really, really bothers me when all some people out there do is try to tear others down. There are so many more constructive things that could be done, like minding one's own business. There are always those people who just like to talk about everyone, and it's not usually anything very nice. They will either directly or in passive-aggressive fashion degrade any detail of the person they are trying to break down. These individuals find something about them, whether it is their appearance, something they said, a project they are working on, or an idea they might have, and say things to discredit the person. I prefer to put my energy into helping the people I care about versus trying to destroy the ones I don't. If I don't like someone or disagree with what they are doing, they will probably never know, but I'll also never go out of my way to help them, but enough about them. How can we be better? How can we stop this behavior from happening, and support those who need help? It is easy to want to go after the bully and forget about the person who is being targeted.

Support people who are making a difference, people who are passionate about their work and are supportive of others. If you have a close community of supportive individuals, then it doesn't matter what negative things other people throw at you. There are those who support and see the merit in what you are doing, and you support them. When you become the target of such aggression, there will be a host of people ready to offer you support. One of the most important qualities of a good leader is to be there for people, showing up, and holding space.

If you find yourself being overly critical of others, it may be because you are being too hard on yourself. Well-meant advice can quickly become an unwanted attack, so remembering to give yourself and other people a break will make you more easygoing and less concerned with what other people are doing. Criticizing others often comes from a place of insecurity, and if we are being self-reflective individuals, it is important to ask why we are so bothered. Is it the actual context, or are we somehow threatened by this person because they represent something we wish we were or a part of ourselves that we want to repress?

Find your passion and your purpose. When you are doing something you love and truly feel passionate about, there is little room for anything else. It is difficult to be concerned about what others say and do when you are living to your fullest potential. Competition becomes camaraderie when you can share that passion with another person. The scarcity mindset causes people to act as if they are in survival mode, especially when it comes to their livelihood or their concept of reality; when either become threatened, people can become vicious. The universe is eternally abundant, and when we are flowing with this energy, our creative potential is unleashed.

Remove the toxin. Some individuals have nothing but venomous vitriol to spew on the rest of us, and we have been taught to turn the other cheek and allow these people space in our lives. I am here to tell you, that is not the only option. Removing toxic people from your life and your surroundings is the ultimate form of self-care and self-sovereignty. I realize that we are not always in a position to hit the Block button in our day-to-day lives, but we have much more control than we realize. If the toxin cannot be removed, it can be neutralized, transmuted into something useful.

The energy that we would like to put in to pointing out exactly why these people are wrong, and what makes them toxic, is better spent on the betterment of ourselves and the people around us. There is no better motivation than not only proving a naysayer wrong, but showing them just how capable you are. There is a reason these people try to tear others down in the first place, and it's because they sense the difference in elevation. They feel the only way to get close to where you are is by pulling you down to them. Hold your ground, and remember that you contain everything that got you where you are in the first place.

It is one thing to disagree with someone, and it is another to antagonize them simply because you dislike them, or they hurt your ego. We don't have to voice every single trespass that has been taken against us, but we also don't have to remain silent if we are being targeted.

Protection from *malocchio*, the evil eye, sounds superstitious, like throwing salt over your shoulder, but one thing I have learned from being on social media is that it is very, very real. We put so much of ourselves and our personal lives out on the internet for public consumption, giving people a window into our lives at that moment. Through this sympathetic connection, we unknowingly make ourselves, our homes, and our livelihood susceptible to the malefic energy of others. Some would call it jealousy, but I think it goes deeper than that. The most powerful evil eyes are formed within deeply dissatisfied individuals. Even people you normally have a good relationship with can cast this influence over your life, and that is why boundaries and protection are so important.

We've all probably experienced feeling envious when something amazing happens to someone close to us, especially if it is something we wanted ourselves. We love and care about that person, but deep down inside, we can't help but feel we deserve it more. It is normal to feel this way, and this is just part of the residual energy we are exposed to on a regular basis. Being conscious of this and keeping yourself protected while not falling into the same trap will get you far.

There are countless ways to protect against the evil eye, and similar concepts can be found in multiple cultures. Simply, wearing an eye-shaped necklace or ring can protect against this, and remind us that critics are always watching. Drawing an eye between you and your device's screen is also an easy way to put up some energetic protection, not only against the evil eye, but also to keep from having a negative reaction yourself.

So, just be nice to people! Remember that another person's success doesn't diminish your own, and that a difference of opinions shouldn't shake the foundations of your world. It's okay to be different, and it's possible for everyone to be happy.

Calming the Magickal Fire

Jaime Gironés

As a Leo, I'm constantly on fire, and the fire can make me enthusiastic, passionate, or creative. But, it can also make me be stubborn, aggressive, dominant, or explosive.

When my fire becomes unstable, it can affect my personal life; I can speak mean words to my partner when I'm angry. It can also affect my work life; I can suddenly realize I've been acting dominant in meetings, not allowing others to say their opinion or thoughts. And it can also affect my magickal and spiritual life: too much passion can influence my spell results, causing radical consequences; too much enthusiasm when engaging within the magickal community can cause me burnout; too much energy in a group ritual can cause me and others overwhelm. If I'm not careful and don't have constant care of my fire, it may grow. And the more it grows, the harder it is to calm down.

I say "calm down" and not "put down" because it is not my intention to cease my fire. My fire allows me to do and accomplish amazing things. But just as a fireplace can be relaxing, a fire can also bring a house or the whole block down in minutes and have people running away from it. I try to turn it down to a level that does not affect me or others.

The most appropriate and efficient way of ceasing the magickal fire is cooling, by bringing the temperature down with water. It can be seen symbolically, as cooling a "hot" situation, or physically (my body temperature is usually very high!). When I am stressed, tired, or burned out, I usually go to places with water: a house with a pool, a river, or the beach.

As a regular practice, I use my shower time to bring my heat down a notch, besides it being a moment for physically and energetically cleansing. Here is a way to calm the magickal fire with water during your daily or regular routine in the shower or bath, or even by taking water with your hands from the faucet.

Bring your attention to your body and focus on the parts that feel hotter or warmer.

Reflect on which parts of the body are hotter, what they could mean, what the trigger could be. Is it the head? Are your thoughts on fire? Is it the stomach? Are you angry? Is it your hands? Are they tired and need a break from creating?

Once you localize the heated area and think of the possible fuel behind it, allow the water to run over it or touch it.

While feeling the water, tell yourself and the heat something like the following: "Thank you, Fire, that shines and heats through me. I am aware of this fuel [here you can name the actual situation or trigger]. I release it and allow my fire to calm down. I'm chill."

A BRIEF BIO OF ANN MOURA

* * *

Ivo Dominguez, Jr.

Ann Moura, who was born August 20, 1947, has written a dozen books on witchcraft—the most recent of which is *Green Witchcraft IV: Walking the Faerie Path*—created the *Green Witch Tarot*, and taught extensively in the United States and overseas. She is one of the few writers I know of who is truly a hereditary witch. Her mother and grandmother were Brazilians of Spanish descent who taught her folk magick, working the spirits of nature and the dead, and much more. Her father, who was of English and German descent, had a profound love of the natural world that he shared with her. She took what she'd been taught by her family, dusted off the Christian names and symbolism that had accumulated over the generations, and created her own path. Her public craft name is Aoumiel, and her Green Witchcraft tradition has inspired many solitaries to find their path.

She is highly accomplished in other parts of her life as well. She holds a bachelor's and a master's degree in history and has been certified as an archivist. She has been a high school teacher, a US Navy lieutenant, and currently owns a metaphysical shop called Luna Sol Esoterica in Florida, which she runs with her daughter Xyn. She also writes poetry; creates art in acrylics, watercolors, and ink; and makes magickal items, such as black mirrors and charm pouches. She has lived all over the United States and has traveled the world.

Ann Moura has many interests, works hard, is a strong individualist, and displays her Leo nature by shining brightly and warmly. Her pursuit of her path, passions, and avocations helps others grow, which is the hallmark of a truehearted Leo. She is no longer traveling to gatherings and conferences, but she continues to write and to provide a resource to her community through her shop.

A Sampling of Leo Occultists

HELENA PETROVNA BLAVATSKY
occultist and writer
(August 12, 1831)

DEMETRA GEORGE
astrologer, classicist, and author
(July 25, 1946)

LADY FRIEDA HARRIS
artist and creator of *Thoth Tarot*
(August 13, 1877)

HELENE KOPPEJAN
founder of The Glastonbury
Experience Centre in England
(August 20, 1927)

JULIA PARKER
astrologer and writer
(July 27, 1932)

RACHEL POLLACK
tarotist and science fiction,
comics, and occult writer
(August 17, 1945)

THE SWAY OF YOUR MOON SIGN

Ivo Dominguez, Jr.

The Moon is the reservoir of your emotions, thoughts, and all your experiences. The Moon is your subconscious, your unconscious, and your instinctive response in the moment. The Moon is also the author, narrator, and the musical score in the ongoing movie in your mind that summarizes and mythologizes your story. The Moon is like a scrying mirror, a sacred well, that gives answers to the question of the meaning of your life. The style and the perspective of your Moon sign shapes your story, a story that starts as a reflection of your Sun sign's impetus. The remembrance of your life events is a condensed subjective story, and it is your Moon sign that summarizes and categorizes the data stream of your life.

In witchcraft, the Moon is our connection and guide to the physical and energetic tides in nature, the astral plane, and other realities. The Moon in the heavens as it moves through signs and phases also pulls and pushes on your aura. The Moon in your birth chart reveals the intrinsic qualities and patterns in your aura, which affects the form your magick takes. Your Sun sign may be the source of your essence and power, but your Moon sign shows how you use that power in your magick. This chapter describes the twelve possible arrangements of Moon signs with a Leo Sun and what each combination yields.

♈

Moon in Aries

Having your Sun and Moon in fire signs ramps up your desire to shine brighter than anyone else. Your abundant creativity and spontaneity are complemented with equal measures of style and charisma. All this can lead you to be a leader and a trendsetter. You don't mind taking chances and you can make decisions quickly. You do have to work on learning detachment from outcomes and becoming more self-observant. Your competitive drive and need for approval from others can get out of balance and cause you difficulties. Taking time to think things through will save you time and trouble in the end.

Courage is something you value in yourself and others. Even when you disagree with someone's beliefs, if they are ardent in following their truth, you will feel respect for their daring choices while strongly disagreeing. This can create some friction in your life, though explaining your reasons will help others better understand your position. You tend to speak with great surety and authority, which can be interpreted as arrogance. Try not to take offense and draw on your Leo Sun's capacity for charm and diplomacy to be a better leader. Let your fire be one that warms rather than roasts and you'll be more effective at reaching your goals.

When it comes to matters of love and friendship, you come on strong. Slow down a bit and let others catch up with how you are feeling. You have a big heart and love to shower affection on others.

Just make sure that you do so with both words and deeds.

An Aries Moon easily stretches forth to connect with the energy of other beings. Your fiery qualities cleanse and protect your aura from picking up other people's emotional debris or being influenced by your environment. It is relatively easy for you to blend your energy with others and to separate cleanly. However, take care not to use up too much of your own energy or burn yourself out. Learning to sense your flow and to moderate it is essential. The energy field and magick of an Aries Moon tends to move and change faster than any other sign, but it is harder to hold to a specific task or shape. This can be overcome with self-awareness and practice.

♉

Moon in Taurus

Both your Sun and Moon are in fixed elements, which gives you steadfastness and a resolute nature. This can help you be more practical and determined but can also lead to an inflexibility that can get in the way of your goals and happiness. The more you learn to cooperate with others, the better. You have great stamina and creativity, but don't try to do everything by yourself. You have a far-reaching grasp of how the world works and you are happiest when you have abundance in your life. Scarcity or concerns for stability can nag at you and wear you down. Have faith that you will get what you need, and though you have perseverance, the most important quality you need to develop is patience.

This Moon encourages you to stop and smell the roses. Allow yourself to revel in your Moon's Taurean sensuality. In astrology, the Moon is said to be exalted in Taurus, which means that it favors success and good fortune. For a Leo, this combination also gives you more creativity in the arts and practical matters. You have an innate sense of how to create an atmosphere, event, or place that encourages others to enjoy the beauty of being alive. Creating an experience you can share with others is the best medicine for you when you are feeling stuck in your life. Procrastination is a big warning sign that you need to recharge your connection to the things that bring you joy and purpose.

A Taurus Moon generates an aura that is magnetic and pulls energy inward. You are good at raising energy for yourself and others in workings and rituals. This Moon also makes it easier to create strong shields and wards. If something does breach your shields or create some other type of energetic injury, get some healing help or the recovery may take longer than it should. Generally, people with a Taurus Moon have less flexibility in their aura. You can work toward improving your flexibility, but the quick fix is to create new boundaries or a larger container. Astral travel and other forms of soul travel are harder to begin with this Moon sign, so draw upon your Leo fire to overcome this. However, once in motion, a stronger and more solid version of you travels than is true for most witches.

♊
Moon in Gemini

Leo's personal magnetism combined with Gemini's gift for communication gives you style, flair, and an influential voice. Your words and actions easily shift between being serious, funny, charming, and inspiring, and you need to take care that your sharp wit doesn't cut too deeply. When you choose to be heard, there are few who can stop you. Your excitement and big ideas are infectious and affect everyone near you. You do enjoy being in the spotlight, and its bright light does tend to follow you, so make sure you are using that attention for good purposes. A Gemini Moon encourages spontaneity and a wide and ever-expanding collection of interests to feed your curiosity. This is exciting and fun, but try to return to tasks that were left unfinished. Your longer-term dreams can only come true if you stay focused and on track. Ask yourself why you are doing what you are doing and if it leads somewhere useful.

Gemini gives you more adaptability than most Leos so you can fit into many settings. Both signs love fun, so be careful not to overbook yourself. Leo likes to go forward at full speed, but a Gemini Moon makes you nimble so that you can swerve and change course. The key to making this Sun-Moon combination work is to form the habit of reminding yourself of your goals so you can get back on track.

Cultivating patience is essential, not just for your projects, but also for how you deal with others.

A Gemini Moon, like all the air Moons, makes it easier to engage in soul travel and psychism and gives the aura greater flexibility. You are a quicksilver fire that seeks connection but not a merger with other beings and energies. When your aura reaches out and touches something, it can quickly read and copy the patterns it finds. A Gemini Moon gives the capacity to quickly adapt and respond to changing energy conditions in working magick or using the psychic senses. However, turbulent spiritual atmospheres are felt strongly and can be uncomfortable or cause harm. A wind can pick up and carry dust and debris, and the same is true for an aura. If you need to cleanse your energy, become still, and the debris will simply fall out of your aura.

Moon in Cancer

This combination has the two brightest of celestial lights in the signs they rule. They encourage you to be loving, compassionate, gallant, and generous with the people around you. You have high ideals and deep instincts, and a great deal of common sense. Your head and your heart are on good speaking terms with each other. You get joy from seeing the ones you care about succeed, which is admirable. You have great potential that may not be realized unless you direct enough focus into your own aspirations and needs. The Leo need to be seen combined with a Cancer Moon means you need true closeness and intimacy with people to be genuinely content. You are good at smiling and putting on a good face, which makes you good company, but you deserve to feel loved, so show your true feelings.

You know what will do well, go viral, and attract public interest. This can serve you in business, politics, the arts, religion, or whatever else you like. You have a creativity that knows how to put people, things, and ideas together for the best possible impact. The Cancer Moon needs stability, which will generally mean a need for financial security. Cancer makes you want a comfortable home and Leo wants to add beauty and style to your surroundings. You'll feel better about life if you invest the time and effort to create your personal sanctuary. If you don't have a splendid and inviting place to live, your negative traits are more likely to come to the surface.

A Cancer Moon gives the aura a magnetic pull that wants to merge with whatever is nearby. Imagine two drops of water growing closer until they barely touch and how they pull together to become one larger drop. The aura of a person with a Cancer Moon is more likely to retain the patterns and energies that it touches. This can be a good thing or a problem depending on what is absorbed. You must cleanse and purify yourself before and after magickal work whenever possible. Fire is your best tool for cleansing yourself. One of the gifts that comes with this Moon is a capacity for healing touch that offers comfort while filling in and healing disruptions in other people's energy.

♌

Moon in Leo

Double the solar fire means that you can be the life of any party and that you are always noticed by people. You do have to be careful that your flamboyance and desire for extravagance don't overwhelm people. It is easy for you to take charge and take up more space than you should. Although you are inherently confident, you do crave regular validation from others. The more you shift the center of praise and focus to others, the more you will be seen as the magnificent being you are. You are strong-willed, idealistic, and have big dreams, so when you are focused on achieving, you may miss out on the fact that your fiery presence is burning the people around you. Learn to take a beat and to read the room to see if you need to cool things down.

You know how to have fun and enjoy life with gusto. Underneath all that boisterous energy, there is a great deal of introspection and a search for higher purpose. You want your life to mean something, and you will set your feelings and everyone else's feelings aside to reach whatever pinnacle of accomplishment you are seeking. This can be seen as a cold aspect to your nature, but it is really white-hot purpose. To keep life in balance, regularly ask yourself if you are being kind and generous. Your best legacy will be how you made people feel, not the many goals you have realized.

A Leo Moon easily stretches forth to connect with the energy of other beings, though a little bit less than Aries and Sagittarius Moons. The fiery qualities cleanse and protect your aura from picking up other people's emotional debris or from being influenced by your environment. It is relatively easy for you to blend your energy with others and to separate cleanly. The Leo Moon also makes it easier for you to find your center and stay centered. The fixed fire of Leo makes it easier to hold large amounts of energy that can be applied for individual and collective workings. You are particularly well suited to ritual leadership or being the primary shaper of energy in a working. You also have a gift for summoning or banishing spirits.

♍

Moon in Virgo

This is a complicated and contradictory mixture of influences. The Virgo Moon is reserved, inward focused, and a planner while your Leo Sun craves adventures, following hunches, and expressing itself publicly. There are many other points of difference between the two signs' basic styles. When you find your way to the midpoint between the two signs, you have the best of both. Virgo's attention to detail and foresight help make those Leo dreams come true. Leo's passion, confidence, and social savvy transform Virgo's self-criticism into a tool for personal growth. When you don't find or maintain this equilibrium, you may find yourself blocked from making decisions—you may push away the people you need, or use arrogance as a self-defense. This sounds challenging, but when you are in your sweet spot, you are regal, inspiring, and amazingly competent. Your observational and analytical skills are every sharp.

This combo brings out the most independent and individualistic traits of both signs. Although you know the rules of society and etiquette, part of you takes glee in breaking those rules. This can be fun, but you'll get more joy from examining the rules you place upon yourself. You are often stricter with yourself than is wise. You are deeply principled and speak your truth no matter the cost. Your personal honor is important to you and can lead to conflicts. Since you are likely to be blunt at times, learn ways to patch up or reweave the bonds that get frayed.

A Virgo Moon generates an aura that is magnetic and pulls energy inward. This Moon also makes it easier to create strong thoughtforms and energy constructs. You have strong shields, but if breached, your shields will tend to lock in the pattern of the injury; get some healing help or the recovery may take longer than it should. Virgo Moons are best at perceiving and understanding patterns and process in auras, energy, spells, and so on. You can be quite good at spotting what is off and finding a way to remedy the situation. This gives the potential to do healing work and curse breaking among other things. This Moon's mutable earth combined with the fixed fire of Leo can give you insights into the mysteries of plants and animals.

♎
Moon in Libra

You have a gift for finding joy and beauty in life. Both signs have a love of art and the sensual pleasures, and you try to see the best in other people. You know how to be a friend and how to show that you care. Your positive stance on the world is not always realistic, more aspirational, but this allows you to better the world by trying to make the ideal into the real. When the world disappoints you, it takes some effort to find your way back to your proper balance. Listen to everyone; it is all information, but it only becomes wisdom after you've placed it into context. Find support within yourself and not in the words others offer. You are drawn to being in charge but hate hurting feelings, which is almost inevitable. You also have a talent for diplomacy, so strengthen your mediation skills and leadership roles will be more comfortable.

You see worlds of nuances in the simplest of things. You are especially sensitive for a Leo and have layers of meaning and thought attached to your emotional inner world. People are attracted to you, charmed by you, and often they think they understand what you are experiencing. More often than not, they've only caught a glimpse of you. You are likely to have as many people as you want in your life, but to have an inner circle that truly sees you, you'll need to do more. Try letting people know that you are also sentimental and a true romantic at heart. Be mindful that your friendly and generous energy may be misunderstood as a positive response to someone's flirtation. Be clear and verbalize your boundaries, needs, and intentions.

A Libra Moon makes it easier to engage in soul travel and psychism and gives the aura greater flexibility. When you are working well with your Libra Moon, you can make yourself a neutral and clear channel for information from spirits and other entities. You are also able to tune in to unspoken requests when doing divinatory work. The auras of people with Libra Moon are very capable at bridging and equalizing differences between the subtle bodies of groups of people. This allows you to bring order and harmony to energies raised and shaped in a group ritual. You may have a talent for writing affirmations, invocations, oaths, and petitions to spirits.

♏

Moon in Scorpio

You have an intensely passionate nature with a desire to take on the world and be tested. Fixed fire plus fixed water tends to make everything feel strongly personal. When you apply that drive to reaching your goals, nothing can stop you. This combination gives great fortitude and determination. When you use that energy to rant, preach, or engage in conflict with trolls, you miss out on all the things you could have accomplished instead. Learn to walk away from the battles that don't matter or cause losses even when you win. You are very independent and often assume you are right. You often are right in your assessments, but not always. Your personal growth depends on expanding your perspective to include facts and perspectives that are new to you.

You're more likely to run with your intuition and then flesh out your plans once you are in motion. This gives you a head start and makes you the frontrunner in whatever goal you choose. You'd do well in business and management, but don't forget to follow your creative urges, even if they are not your livelihood. You have a strong survival instinct, which means that sometimes you will put your principles aside and choose pragmatism. This can stir up trouble, and you'll need to work on managing how people see you. The Scorpio Moon puts up a wall around you so that you need to make a choice to laugh and let people see your lighter side. Otherwise, people will peg you as serious, mysterious, and unapproachable. Turn on that Leo charisma. This combo tends toward higher stress levels, and positive interactions with people are your best medicine.

A Scorpio Moon gives the aura a magnetic pull that wants to merge with whatever is nearby. You easily absorb information about other people, spirits, places, and so on. If you are not careful, the information and the emotions will loop and repeat in your mind. To release what you have picked up, acknowledge what you perceive and then reframe its meaning in your own words. The magick of a Scorpio Moon is adept at probing and moving past barriers, shields, and wards. This also gives you the power to remove things that should not be present. Leo's fire mixed with Scorpio's water also grants the capacity to read the energy of objects and places.

↗

Moon in Sagittarius

A lion-centaur hybrid means that your need for stimulation is almost constant. You want to travel, explore realms of thought, go on an adventure, plot world domination, or at least create a webzine, and race Peter Pan across the sky. Geeking out on your newest favorite interest and telling the world it is amazing is one of your signature moves. All fields of knowledge, culture, and art catch your attention. You have an abundance of enthusiasm, optimism, and energy to pursue your dreams and interests. You are outspoken and would have a hard time bottling up your thoughts or feelings. Your Leo nature mixed with a Sagittarius Moon leads you to shine your light by showing others all the possibilities the world has to offer. You don't have as much of a need to be in the spotlight as most Leos so long as what you are doing is exciting or has personal meaning.

Your weak spot is following through when your plans require many steps or consistent effort. Develop planning skills, time management skills, and reward yourself when you accomplish tasks. It is not likely that these behaviors will take root naturally, so you must choose to foster them and reinforce them. You do like punctuality; this may arise from impatience or from wanting to move on to whatever comes next. You are highly adaptable and quick-witted, so even if you drop the ball occasionally, you'll pick it up and recover. You are a bit of a perfectionist, so you are often happier when you are the boss or left to do things your way. If you are being blocked by someone, turn on your warmth, charm, and the twinkle in your eye, and most people will let you get your way.

The auras of people with Sagittarius Moon are the most adaptable of the fire Moons. Your energy can reach far and change its shape easily. You are particularly good at affecting other people's energy or the energy of a place. Like the other fire Moons, your aura is good at cleansing itself, but it is not automatic and requires your conscious choice. This is because the mutable fire of Sagittarius is changeable and can go from a small ember to a pillar of fire that reaches the sky. It is important that you manage your energy so it is somewhere between the extremes of almost extinguished and furious inferno. Your health depends on proper energy management.

♑

Moon in Capricorn

This earthy Moon provides an excellent vessel to house and focus Leo's fire. You have a strong sense of purpose and enough self-discipline to tackle almost anything. You are more serious and self-sufficient than most Leo Sun people. You still have much of the warmth and charm of a Leo, but you project a hard strength as well. The velvet glove comes off quickly to reveal an iron hand when something opposes your goals. Much of your success comes from the planning, plotting, and analysis that a Capricorn Moon loves. The downside to this gift is that you can be too serious, and your Leo Sun needs to have fun to stay healthy. Schedule time for recreation or it won't happen often enough. You also are prone to being too harsh a critic of your own efforts.

This can wear down your innate Leo sense of self-worth. Cut yourself some slack and you'll improve faster.

Over time, people will grow to admire you and what you've accomplished. Some may be cautious around you because you have a glare that can kill. Be mindful of how big an impact that your moods have on others. Your personal standards apply to you and not to others. You'll have fewer unnecessary conflicts when you understand people on their own terms. If you do need something to change, try persuasion first rather than transforming your magnetic charm into a coercion. You need a partner who can go toe to toe with you. Mutual support and reciprocity are essential to happiness in your relationships. You are unlikely to have a normal personal life, and that is okay. Create a home and a family of choice that suits you, not what society tries to enforce.

A Capricorn Moon generates an aura that is magnetic and pulls energy inward. What you draw to yourself tends to stick and solidify, so be wary, especially when doing healing work or cleansings. The magick of a Capricorn Moon is excellent at imposing a pattern or creating a container in a work-ing. Your spells and workings tend to be durable. You also have a knack for building wards and doing protective magick. With proper training, you are good at manifesting the things you need. Fire con-tained by this earthy Moon also gives you remark-able stamina in workings and rituals.

Moon in Aquarius

This combination produces an inventive, resource-ful, and lively mind. In addition to a keen intellect, you also have strong intuition that counterbalances your thought process. You tend to examine your own life, feelings, and motivations more than most Leos. You need a bit more solitude than the average Leo to stay on an even keel. Your imagination is power-ful, and if you can create it in your mind, you can find a way to make it happen in the world. You have an aptitude for finding the steps that transform an idea into a reality. Aquarius makes you more idealistic and ideological, which, when combined with Leo's desire for self-expression, can lead to monologues or rants depending on the listener's perspective. Take care that you pick the right time, place, and audience for these passionate speeches so that you will inspire people rather than rub them the wrong way. You are a good storyteller, and stories often work better than rhetoric.

You'd do well as a teacher, counselor, coach, or in any situation that calls for imparting knowledge and helping people find their personal best. You love to look for deeper meanings in everything. Most people with this combination value diversity of every kind and are champions for creating a more open society. You do good work as an individual but do even better in groups where you act as the catalyst that pulls it all together. You are loving and warmhearted, but you tend to live at a fast pace. Make sure you find partners and close friends who can keep up or learn to look back and check on them.

Your Aquarius Moon encourages a highly mobile and flexible aura. Without a strong focus, the power of an air subtle body becomes scattered and diffuse. If you have an air Moon, an emphasis should be placed on finding and focusing on your center of energy. Grounding is important, but focusing on your core and center is more important. From that center, you can strengthen and stabilize your power. People with Aquarius Moon are good at shaping and holding a specific thoughtform or energy pattern and transferring it to other people or into objects. The fiery energy of Leo also allows you to project your thoughts, feelings, images, and so on for significant distances.

♓

Moon in Pisces

Although these signs are very different, fixed fire and mutable water, when used well, bring out the best in each other. You are worldly and spiritual with an enchanting personality and presence. You are forceful when you need to be but also as yielding as water when it serves better. You need to guard your heart because you feel deeply and are easily and equally hurt by thoughtless actions or intentional cruelty to yourself or what you observe. Thicken your skin and put up some shields, but don't harden your beautiful heart. You do better when you have lots of people in your life. A circle of friends is your best defense and medicine against the harshness of the world.

You would like the world to be more honorable and straightforward than it is. Occasionally you do need a personal quest, a walkabout, or perhaps just a regular yoga or meditation session to rebalance your fire and water natures.

You have deep wellsprings of creativity that can be applied in the arts, the sciences, or in business. You would also do well in health care. If you don't have enough opportunity for self-expression or block the flow, it can turn into fretting and brooding. When you lose your balance, this combo creates dramatic emotional states and poor choices. Doing charitable work, being a volunteer, or serving your community helps recenter and ground you. Your physical health also relies on keeping yourself in equilibrium. You are ambitious, and there is nothing wrong with that, so embrace it so you don't create stress overthinking it.

With a Pisces Moon, the emphasis should be on learning to feel and control the rhythm of your energetic motion in your aura. Water Moon sign auras are flexible, cohesive, and magnetic, so they tend to ripple and rock like the action of waves. Pisces Moon is the most likely to absorb and hang on to unwanted emotions or energies. Rippling your energy and bouncing things off the outer layers of your aura is a good defense. Be careful, develop good shielding practices, and make cleansing yourself and your home a regular practice. The energy of people with Pisces Moon is best at energizing, comforting, and healing disruptions in other people's auras. Your Leo energy helps you use this Moon to cast illusions, create stealth work, and reveal hidden spiritual influences.

TAROT
CORRESPONDENCES
♌

You can use the tarot cards in your work as a Leo witch for more than divination. They can be used as focal points in meditations and trance to connect with the power of your sign or element or to understand it more fully. They are great on your altar as an anchor for the powers you are calling. You can use the Minor Arcana cards to tap into Saturn, Jupiter, or Mars in Leo energy even when they are in other signs in the heavens. If you take a picture of a card, shrink the image and print it out; you can fold it up and place it in spell bags or jars as an ingredient.

Leo Major Arcana

Strength

All the Fire Signs

The Ace of Wands

Aries Minor Arcana

5 of Wands	Saturn in Leo
6 of Wands	Jupiter in Leo
7 of Wands	Mars in Leo

MY MOST LEO WITCH MOMENT

Coby Michael

Trying to think of something for this one took me to some dark places for a sign ruled by the Sun. I could delve into the depths of what it's like when your Sun is eclipsed and your life falls into darkness, but I am more interested in the rest of the story. There have been enough clouds in my sky. Despite my own personal struggles, I have always been able to find the beauty in the world. Sometimes I would find it in places where no one else wanted to look.

I have been an artist since I could hold a pencil. I used to obsessively draw the tiniest circles I possibly could over and over again before I could even write. Drawing, painting, and photography have been lifelong interests of mine, and I have always been able to pick up on various creative mediums with ease. I am a creator, and that is my Most Leo Witch Moment. I create things to help and inspire people, and to make them happy. Sometimes I create things just because they are pretty. I do it because it makes me feel good.

Beauty and aesthetic have always played a large role in my life. I grew up raised mostly by Libras. My mother is a cosmetologist, and I worked in the beauty industry for ten years. For me, there is nothing more magickal and divine than creating beauty. This is, of course, entirely subjective, but it is no different than having a client in your chair and seeing the look in their eyes when you make them look like they did during a time in their life when they felt beautiful. Or maybe they are seeing that beauty for the first time. Beauty is not on the surface. It radiates like the Sun from within, shining on everything around them. True beauty isn't seen with the eyes. It is felt by the heart.

I create in lots of different ways. I make herbal formulas, ritual jewelry, and other occult artifacts for my job, and all of these have their own unique beauty. Even the sinister and baneful plants I work with are made into beautiful talismanic jewelry and oils that shine like emeralds. One thing I have learned from living a life obscured by various shadows is that there is beauty in the dark places too. Everyone and everything wants to be loved, and that is why I create—to show my love.

I want people to remember that we are powerful, beautiful, and worthy. If I can create something that helps someone get to that place, I will do it a thousand times over. The things that I create are meant to empower people, to show them that they can take back their lives, their bodies, themselves.

It has taken me such a long time to get to a place where I wasn't living in survival mode. I didn't let myself live for many years because I was desperately trying to make it to where I needed to. I forgot how I liked to dress, what foods I enjoyed most, and what I liked to do for fun when I wasn't working. It took so much to overcome the obstacles in my way that I had to be a warrior for myself. I became hardened, but even then I could still find beauty.

Coming out of trauma, addiction, and abuse left me with very little self-confidence or sense of sovereignty in my life, but I knew I had a purpose, and all I could do was move toward it. I think back over the years, and the low places I was in mentally, but all that time I was still creating, making people beautiful and teaching other people how to do the same. I never stopped, and it brings tears to my eyes writing about it. We can still be in a dark place and create beauty. We can still shine our light on the world even if we are lost in the shadows.

From where I sit now, I can see it all laid out before me, and there is nothing more beautiful, even the painful parts. There is no greater masterpiece than the life we paint for ourselves. I have confidence because I can finally confide in myself. I can look in the mirror and see the beauty that has been there all along, and that realization is my greatest gift.

I will always create and make the world a more beautiful place while I am here. Through my experiences I seek to empower others, to show up for them, and to see their beauty. It is my hope that through my creations—whether jewelry, relationships, or space for community—that a little spark of what is in me will ignite in others what is within them.

Leo Witch SELF Altar

Nothing could possibly be more Leo than creating a personal shrine to ourselves. If any other signs are reading this, I'm sure they will be thinking how typical this is, and that's the beauty of it. It taps into our already strong sense of a connection to Self, strengthening that connection and working to empower ourselves to manifest our desires. This shrine is a place for you, and you alone. I have mine in my bedroom where no one else will bother it.

It is up to you what you put on this shrine and how you adorn it because it is yours. Having a photo of yourself on the altar and other meaningful objects—candles in your favorite color, charms, talismans, and other tools of empowerment—is a good place to start. This space will be the focus of all rituals of self-love, empowerment, protection, and manifestation of your personal desires.

My personal shrine has a photo of me when I was a teenage goth kid, and I had just come out of the closet and felt very protective of myself at that point. This idea started as a way to heal my inner child and celebrate that part of myself still being with me. Older me wants to honor that boy from long ago and send him healing and protection from the present. My bedroom has almost always been decorated in black and another color. Currently it is black and red because those colors are dramatic and sexy. The colors are also for protection, passion, and power. I have a number of special ritual items that I have been given that also have a place there, as well as my tarot cards. The central space of the altar changes accordingly to specific intentions or goals that I am focusing on, or energies that I want to bring into my life.

This can be a place of meditation and devotion to self-care, working with this altar after ritual baths, and to cast glamour spells. This can be a bedside altar to bear witness to ecstatic rites of a sexual nature. By working to empower ourselves, to heal our hearts and embrace our passions, we fill ourselves with potent energy, our vibrations change, and we are better equipped to protect ourselves against psychic attack, energy drain, and other environmental factors.

Invoking Confidence

David Salisbury

It's nine in the morning and I'm seated in an overstuffed waiting room chair at my doctor's office. As I lean over to investigate the stack of old magazines on the end table next to me, I notice a little framed sign. You know the type; signs with random inspirational quotes you see in waiting rooms and classrooms for no particular reason. This one seemed to take on an oracular message as I read it the day I decided what I wanted to write about for this book. "Doubt kills more dreams than failure ever will."

What an excellent way to frame the power of confidence. Confidence is one of the greatest gifts given to us by Leo, whether naturally occurring in our astrological charts or invoked for practical use. When we lack skill, experience, or even circumstantial odds, confidence can sometimes be relied upon entirely to push our goals forward. Although some people seem to naturally embody a healthy sense of confidence (and you'll often find those of us with our Sun in Leo fit that), everyone could use more of it at times. To "invoke confidence" means that we dare to act amid uncertainty. To align with action, we will invoke confidence through movement and by drawing down one of the rays of power that comes to us from the Theosophical traditions. Feel free to adapt the movements here to your personal ability. The idea is to start out in a low position and then rise up as best as you can.

Lie on your back on the ground, breathing slow and deep with your eyes closed. Imagine the meekest, most incapable version of yourself. In this state, you are small, looking up at the world and all its opportunities in the distance. Within that far distance, you see a blazing red sun shining and sending its rays forth. Imagine those rays coalescing and forming a single red ray that hits your chest and sets your body aglow.

Slowly turn over and rise until you're seated on your knees. Imagine your body growing bigger, fueled by this red ray of action and will. This solar power fills you, and you sense a red flame dancing across the edges of your skin on all your limbs.

Rise from your knees and form a standing position. The ray continues to shoot forth as you imagine your body becoming bigger than the space you occupy. As you become bigger, you realize that those distant opportunities are now easily within your grasp.

Stretch your arms upward to the sky and feel the red power causing you to become larger than the Earth itself, matching the size of the sun that fuels you. You can accompany this position by speaking aloud these words of power:

By fixed fire and solar flame, I tie this power to my name.

As the words are spoken, you feel the power of the red ray absorbing slowly into your being and settling comfortably within the body. Remain in this position for another moment, feeling completely aflame with confidence and the will to take the action needed to accomplish your goals.

YOUR RISING SIGN'S INFLUENCE

Ivo Dominguez, Jr.

The rising sign, also known as the ascendant, is the sign that was rising on the eastern horizon at the time and place of your birth. In the birth chart, it is on the left side of the chart on the horizontal line that divides the upper and lower halves of the chart. Your rising sign is also the cusp of your first house. It is often said that the rising sign is the mask you wear to the world, but it is much more than that. It is also the portal through which you experience the world. The sign of your ascendant colors and filters those experiences. Additionally, when people first meet you, they meet your rising sign. This means they interact with you based on their perception of that sign rather than your Sun sign. This in turn has an impact on you and how you view yourself. As they get to know you over time, they'll meet you as your Sun sign. Your ascendant is like the colorful clouds that hide the Sun at dawn, and as the Sun continues to rise, it is revealed.

The rising sign will also have an influence on your physical appearance as well as your style of dress. To some degree, your voice, mannerisms, facial expressions, stance, and gait are also swayed by the sign of your ascendant. The building blocks of your public persona come from your rising sign. How you arrange those building blocks is guided by your Sun sign, but your Sun sign must work with what it has been given. For witches, the rising sign shows some of the qualities and foundations for the magickal personality you can construct. The magickal personality is much more than simply shifting into the right headspace, collecting ritual gear, the lighting of candles, and so on. The magickal persona is a construct that is developed through your magickal and spiritual practices to serve as an interface between different parts of the self. The magickal persona, also known as the magickal personality, can also act as a container or boundary so that the mundane and the magickal parts of a person's life can each have its own space. Your rising also gives clues about which magickal techniques will come naturally to you.

This chapter describes the twelve possible arrangements of rising signs with a Leo Sun and what each combination produces. There are 144 possible kinds of Leo when you take into consideration the Moon signs and rising signs. You may wish to reread the chapter on your Moon sign after reading about your rising sign so you can better understand these influences when they are merged.

♈

Aries Rising

The fire of Leo blends with an Aries rising to push you to be impulsive, exuberant, and brave. Mostly this is a good thing, but a bit of caution and reconnaissance before you leap into something would be wise. This is a forceful combo with high aspirations and tons of energy, but you need to be careful not to burn out. You may not run out of fire, but you will get too crispy around the edges if you don't learn to rein yourself in. Also be cautious that you don't overindulge in life's physical pleasures because you are drawn to excess.

Having the ruling planets of the Sun and Mars means you will radiate sensual, romantic, or at the very least friendly energy that will attract people's attention. This will wax and wane in intensity but is always present. Make sure you let people know your intentions so that there is no misunderstanding. When you lose your cool, this can result in explosive anger. Learn to give small warnings so that people know when to give you space. You want to inspire and guide people, and that will be harder if you seem erratic. You do better when you have trusted friends and companions. They need to know that you care about them, and your words and actions must demonstrate your affection.

An Aries rising means that when you reach out to draw in power, fire will answer quickly and in abundance. If you need other types of energy, you need to reach farther, focus harder, and be more specific in your request. This combination makes it easier for you to summon and call forth spirits and powers and create bindings. The creation of servitors, amulets, and charms is favored as well. This rising also amplifies protective magick for yourself and others.

Taurus Rising

A Taurus rising can bring serenity and steadfast determination that complements Leo's confidence. If you are not vigilant, this can also turn into unreasonable stubbornness and rigidity. Ask yourself whether you are acting with kindness and compassion. Listen to the people you trust when they make observations or give advice. You have a greater need for quiet times and a cozy home than most Leos. Investing in clothing that is comfortable and fits you well is important as it acts as protection as you go about your activities in the world. You love beautiful things, and this love leads to beautiful clutter. Try to declutter by giving things away.

You have good instincts for helping people discover their innate talents. You also know how to put people at ease. Whether it is children or adults, teaching or mentoring will be a part of your life and possibly a profession at times. It is easier for you to talk about other people's emotions, but you are shy when it comes to expressing yours. Working with people teaches you how to show your heart. As you get older, try to maintain or increase your level of physical activity. This is essential if you want to keep that Leo fire bright and your body comfortable.

Taurus rising strengthens your aura and the capacity to maintain a more solid shape to your energy. This gives you stronger shields and allows you to create thoughtforms and spells that are longer lasting. This combination also makes you a better channel for other people's energy in group work because you can tolerate larger volumes of different types of energies. You have a powerful voice for invocations, trance work, and hypnosis. This combo also makes it easier to work with nature spirits and plant spirits in particular.

♊

Gemini Rising

This rising sharpens your Leo communication skills and makes them absolutely bewitching. You are more curious about everything and everyone than most Leos. You come across as bright, vivacious, and genuinely interested in the people around you. This keeps you in the loop for all the events and activities that you want to attend. You do have a fear of missing out that can get out of hand. You'd get closer to achieving your goals if you dug deeper into the details and focused on sticking to your plans. Try knitting, painting, carving, playing a musical instrument, juggling, or anything that uses your hands in a skillful way. These sorts of activities greatly reduce stress and improve mental focus.

You tend to treat your friends as if they were family and your family as if they were friends. Usually this works, but when it doesn't, quickly adjust how you see and treat the person who doesn't like this arrangement. You love being in love, which is a wonderful thing if managed well. Just make sure everyone is on the same page on how you set the rules of your relationship.

Gemini rising combines your Leo creativity to make you adept at writing spells and rituals. This rising helps your energy and aura stretch farther and to adapt to whatever it touches. You would do well to develop your receptive psychic skills as well as practices such as mediumship and channeling. This combination can also lend itself to communication with animals and plants. You can pick up too much information and it can be overwhelming. Learn to close and control your awareness of other people's thoughts and feelings. You may have a gift for interpreting dreams and the words that come from oracles and seers.

Cancer Rising

You are more easily hurt than most Leos, though you still manage to shine and seem untroubled. You show caring through material gestures such as food, gifts, the gift of your time, and the opening of your heart. You don't always feel like others reciprocate and hold up their end of a friendship or relationship. This is true some of the time, but it may also be that you do not understand how others express caring. Leo wants to be known, but your Cancer rising likes to put up a mask to the world. You want to go with your gut most of the time, but that is not a good idea. Choose to use your intellect so you are not ruled by your emotions. An even mix of head and heart will steer you right.

You have a love of history, folklore, genealogy, museums, and such. This can bring you great joy and activities that you treasure your whole life. These interests may shape your career choices. You need to blow your own horn more often. You get things done so smoothly that your efforts aren't always noticed. In matters of love, you also need to be more direct to be thought of as more than a friend.

Cancer grants the power to use your emotions, or the emotional energy of others, to power your witchcraft. Though you can draw on a wide range of energies to fuel your magick, raising power through emotion is the simplest. You may also have a calling for dreamwork or past-life recall. Moon magick works well for you as does work done by the ocean. Color magick—such as the choice of colors for candles, altar cloths, robes, banners—and color visualization can also serve you well.

♌

Leo Rising

When you enter a room, the energy shifts and most people look up. This is great when you feel like taking charge or being the center of attention, but that is not always true. This notice can lead you to success and high goals and often working a bit too hard and long. Try to center yourself, and you and your dear ones will all be happier. Leo is ruled by the Sun, and you tend to create the emotional and spiritual weather around you. When you are not doing well, things turn stormy. Seeing the impact you have on others may lead you to relying on people's reactions and feedback to monitor your state of being. Check in with your inner self instead and you'll be better off.

You love to be over the top on most things in your life. You tend to always think that more is better. This can lead to overspending, and though you have a gift for finding more money, learning to economize is important. You are a loyal friend and tend to forgive offenses swiftly. Be as kind to yourself as you are to others. In matters of love, remind yourself that the first flush of attraction and romance is not mature love. Give yourself time before making commitments.

Leo rising means that when you reach out to draw in power, fire will answer first. If you need other types of energy, you need to reach farther, focus harder, and be more specific in your request. Your aura and energy are brighter and steadier than most people, so you attract the attention of spirits, deities, and so on. Whether or not showing up so clearly in the otherworlds is a gift or a challenge is up to you. Your Sun and rising give you a knack for energy healing work.

♍

Virgo Rising

Virgo greatly tones down the verve and panache of Leo and gives a more serious impression. You are more precise in your word choices and your actions. You are a keen observer of the world who notices the pertinent details. When you are doing well, you are discerning, and when you are frustrated, you become hypercritical. When you are overwrought, your verbal criticisms can cut beyond the bone and all the way to the soul. If you can, walk away when this mood hits and try coming back when you are better controlled. The goal is to be effective in getting what you need, righting a wrong, and so on, and not just blowing off steam.

You are more modest than many Leos, but you do take great pride in your accomplishments and in being good at what you do. You can hold a lot of information in your head at once. It does make you a bit crazy when you must engage in group efforts when you are sure you'd be better off doing it all yourself. You love your freedom, so to have successful close relationships, you need to find people who are comfortable with the amount of space and independence you need. Despite needing space, you still want romance, special gestures of love, cozy getaways, and so on.

Virgo rising with a Leo Sun makes it easier to work with goddesses and gods who are connected to the element of earth, plant life, agriculture, death, or chthonic matters. You have a flair for creating guided visualizations that can work magick. Divination, oracular work, and acting as a voice for spirits are favored. Be careful when you entwine your energy with someone else because you can adopt and retain their patterns and issues. Always cleanse your energy after doing solo or collective work.

♎

Libra Rising

You can become whatever is needed for any situation. You know how to sound, what to wear, and how to pull off all the little nonverbal cues of a culture, scene, or in-group. You can be well bred or raunchy as needed and code-switch at will. It does cost you energy to do this, but it is one of your superpowers. Your warmth can melt away most icy obstacles. Your weakness is that you care too much what people say or think about you. This can derail you from finishing projects or reaching goals. Your quality of life will improve the more you stick to completing your plans.

A messy or unlovely room can dampen your mood faster than an impolite person. The reverse is also true in that beauty feeds you. Make sure you make the spaces that you occupy as harmonious and lovely as you can manage. The more your day-to-day life matches your aesthetics, the more vitality you will have. Also, your environment changes your moods, so controlling your environment goes a long way toward evening out your moods.

Libra rising with a Leo Sun wants to express its magick through the creation of things. You may carve and dress candles and create sumptuous altars, healing poppets, or amazing ritual wear. You also know how to bring together people who use different types of magick and arrange smooth collaborations. You are good at helping others cut energetic cords and release spiritual or emotional attachments that no longer are healthy. Working with sound in magick and healing, whether it be voice, singing bowls, percussion, or an instrument, is also one of your gifts.

♏

Scorpio Rising

This combination makes for one of the most intense types of Leos. Your allure, air of mystery, and personal power are off the charts. You know what you want, and you will do whatever is needed to get it. When you feel you are right, nothing on Earth can overpower that opinion. If you feel you are blocked from reaching your goals, your frustration can make matters worse. This combination can set up situations that cause you to be seen as domineering or insensitive. Compromise does not come easily to you, but sarcasm does. Like all Leos, your core seeks to illuminate the world. Once, or ideally several, times a day, take deep breaths and recenter yourself. Stay centered and you'll be more effective and have allies and friends.

You are deeply insightful and might do well as a lawyer, a therapist, a writer, and, of course, a witch. You are one of a kind in so many ways and are unforgettable. Leo and Scorpio have different approaches to life, which creates an internal tension that can be a great source of energy or lock you up. Turn the black or white of this tension into shades of gray or, better yet, a full rainbow. Look to the rest of your chart, your life experience, and input from friends to find the nuances so you become more flexible.

Scorpio rising makes your energy capable of pushing through most energetic barriers. You can dissolve illusion or bring down wards or shields and see through to the truth. You may have an aptitude for breaking curses and lifting oppressive spiritual atmospheres. You could be a seer, but only if you learn emotional detachment. You may also have skill as a healer of physical problems. It is important that you do regular cleansing work for yourself. You are likely to end up doing messy work and you do not have a nonstick aura.

♐

Sagittarius Rising

You really are a ray of sunshine that freely shares warmth and optimism. You are among the easiest-going and most flexible of Leos. You are tolerant of other people's foibles and you get real enjoyment from watching others have fun. You are an open book, which is mostly good, though sometimes you overshare or speak the truth too bluntly. The good news is that people are quick to forgive you. You don't know what you can't do, which often results in you accomplishing minor miracles. Don't rest on your laurels for long. Take a victory lap and get back to work.

You love to travel and are equally interested in cultures, landscapes, and meeting new people. When you need to recharge, being outdoors is your best option, whether it be a city park, a backyard, or the seaside—what matters is that you have the sky above. You can feel the interconnectedness of all living things more easily when you are outside. You enjoy being fully present in your body to feel your fires flow. This may be sports, dancing, hiking, or any activity that moves your body and engages your senses. You also feel more alive when you are acting for social justice or a healthier world.

Your magick is stronger when you are standing outside on the ground. Your rising sign's fire can become a pillar of flame in your hearth. Skill in the use of candles, wands, or staves is favored by this combination. This is because you can push your energy and intentions into objects with ease. You have a talent for rituals and spells that call forth creativity, wisdom, and freedom. This combination gives access to lots of energy, but you can crash hard when you run out. Stop before you are tired. If you do astral travel or soul journeying, be sure all of you is back and in its proper place within you.

♑
Capricorn Rising

Ambition is strong in you, and you are methodical and relentless in your pursuit of success. You also have a sense of duty and obligation to serve the needs of your community or society. You are serious and stately, but you are not somber. You enjoy the world as much as any other Leo. You do work harder and play less than most. Your challenge is to make sure you keep a good balance in your life. It is easy for you to get so enthralled with your tasks that you neglect spending quality time with people who care about you. You can go long stretches without too much human contact, but without affection and positive regard, you'll begin to fade.

You know how to take a step back from your feelings and look at situations with more objectivity than most people. This will help when progress is delayed on the tasks you've chosen. Why are there delays? You choose large tasks, and not even you can make time run faster all the time. In your personal life, this can make you an excellent friend or partner—just don't vanish into your work. Also, your partner needs to be very nurturing and wise to the hard façade you put up.

Capricorn rising creates an aura and energy field that is slow to come up to speed, but has amazing momentum once fully activated. Make it your habit to do some sort of energy work or meditative warm-up before engaging in witchcraft. Try working with crystals, stones, even geographic features like mountains as your magick blends well with them. Your rituals and spells benefit from having a structure and a plan of action. You are especially good at warding and spells to make long-term changes. You may have a gift for manipulating the flow of time.

Aquarius Rising

You are always looking for ways that humanity could be doing better and trying to figure out your part in moving things forward. This moves you through a roller coaster of hot and cold emotions that you try to keep hidden. You'll be fine as long as you let them flow and not get stuck on one like anger or disgust, or unrealistic optimism. You will make a difference, but just give people some time to think through all the amazing and practical ideas you have to offer. Your weakness is that you become more rigid when under threat. Little changes in plans or schedules can annoy you to the point of disruption. If you are nimbler and more flexible with your thinking, you'll do better. When you do lose your control and your cool, it is quite a memorable sight for all present.

This combination makes for original thinking and moments of genius. The Leo side of this combination provides the power to make those ideas real. You have a broader understanding of how the large systems of society and business work, so you can apply your talents almost anywhere. When it comes to long-term partners, you need to have an intellectual *and* a physical connection. Your partner will also need to be more adaptable than you are to make things work. It is important that you have some ritual wherein you exchange personally meaningful vows.

Aquarius rising helps you consciously change the shape and density of your aura. This makes you a generalist who can adapt to many styles and forms of magick. Witchcraft focused on calling inspiration, creating community, and personal transformation is supported by this combination. Visualization can play an important role in your magick and meditations. If you aren't particularly good at visualization, then focus your gaze on objects on your altar related to your work. Aquarius rising is gifted at turning ideas into reality.

Pisces Rising

You have a dreamy glow about you that has hints of sunlight glinting on the ocean. There is an otherworldly feel to you. You are so immersed in your psychic perceptions that you can forget you are psychic. On a daily basis you walk as many steps in otherworlds as in this one. You are guided and often protected, but don't make your spirit helpers work too hard. Regardless of what you do in your mundane life, you are a dreamer, a visionary, and a witch by right of instinct. You can excel in a wide range of fields, but the ones that make you feel alive involve providing people with an experience that opens their hearts, minds, or spirits.

Although you may be shy when you are young, over time, your Leo Sun will make you bolder and better able to stand up for yourself. You are affectionate and definitely enjoy romance with all the bells and whistles. When you are in love, you open up completely and are quite vulnerable. You will defend your family until your last breath. Music, and the arts in general, is one of the best medicines for your body, mind, and spirit.

Pisces rising connects your Leo Sun with the other planes of reality. Your power as a witch flows when you do magick to open the gates to the otherworlds. You have a special gift for creating sacred space and blessing places. You can do astral travel, hedge riding, and soul travel in all their forms with some training and practice. You can help others open up their psychic gifts. Music, chanting, and/or dance also fuel your witchcraft. Scrying in water or a crystal ball will serve you well.

A DISH FIT FOR A LEO: ORANGE SUNSHINE CAKE WITH EDIBLE FLOWERS

Dawn Aurora Hunt

* * *

Bursting with flavor and panache, this decadent dessert can be adorned with as much flash and fanfare as can be imagined.

This cake could stop traffic, just like you, Leo. Ruled by the Sun, oranges play the key role in this perfectly balanced dessert. Add charisma to this confection by designing an outstanding look with edible orange flowers like nasturtium and candied orange peels or add drama with purple pansies and clementine slices. Filled with orange curd and liberally frosted with orange-vanilla buttercream, this cake stands out as the individual it is. Share it for parties, celebrations, and anytime you want to make a splashy presentation.

Ingredients:

- 3 cups all-purpose flour or gluten-free flour
- 1½ tablespoons baking powder
- 1½ cups sugar
- ½ teaspoon salt
- 1½ cups unsalted butter, softened
- 4 eggs
- Zest from 1 large orange
- Zest from 1 large lemon
- ¾ cup milk
- ½ cup orange juice
- *For the orange curd:*
    - Juice from 2 large oranges (about ½ cup)
    - Zest from 1 large orange and 1 large lemon
    - 2 eggs
    - 2 egg yolks
    - 1 cup sugar
    - 6 tablespoons butter
- *For the frosting:*
    - 3 tablespoons unsalted butter, softened
    - 2½ cups confectioners' sugar
    - 3 tablespoons orange juice
    - Zest from one orange
    - 1 tablespoon vanilla extract

Directions:

Make the curd. In a medium double boiler, or nonreactive medium saucepan, on medium-low heat, add juice, zest, and sugar and whisk until sugar is dissolved. Reduce heat to low. Gently add the eggs and yolks, stirring constantly with a wooden spoon. Do not whisk or overheat or the eggs will cook too quickly. Stirring constantly, add butter by the tablespoonful, making sure it is completely dissolved before adding more. When the butter has all been melted in and the consistency of the curd is thick enough to coat the back of the spoon, remove it from the heat. Strain the curd through a cheesecloth mesh strainer and set aside covered for about two hours until it comes to room temperature.

Meanwhile, make the cake. Preheat the oven to 350°F. Generously grease two cake pans, nine-inch round. In a large bowl, mix together flour, salt, and baking powder. In a large bowl with an electric mixer, cream together butter and sugar until light and fluffy, cleaning the sides of the bowl down periodically. Beat in the eggs one at a time. Gently beat in milk, juice, and zest until well combined. Add the dry ingredients by the half cup until everything is well combined. Distribute batter evenly in both prepared cake pans and bake for twenty to thirty minutes until cake tests done with a clean toothpick. Let cool completely on wire racks before frosting.

While the cake is cooling, make the frosting. Using an electric mixer with a whisk attachment, beat the butter until fluffy on medium speed. Add the confectioners' sugar by the half cup and cream together. Continue to beat on low while adding the juice, zest, and vanilla. When the frosting is a creamy and spreadable consistency, set aside at room temperature until the cake is also room temperature and ready to frost. Assemble the cake by placing one cake on a cake plate, then liberally piping curd on top of it, layering the next cake on top of the curd. Evenly coat the cake in frosting around the sides and top using a cake spatula or large flat knife. Decorate with edible flowers like nasturtium or pansies. Create elaborate designs using orange slices, clementine slices, or kumquats.

RECHARGING AND SELF-CARE

Coby Michael

Leos are absolute givers. We will give everything if it means we feel loved, needed, and secure, even if this is to our own detriment. It is in our nature to give everything and to do everything, because if we don't, who else will? This also applies to projects we are passionate about. We will often work ourselves past the point of exhaustion, running on nothing but Leo's fire.

Aries can release immense amounts of energy at once, Leo's fire burns long and steady, and Sagittarius can ignite multiple areas at the same time, but all of us have to refuel, and if we don't, we *burn out*! With all the different relationships in our lives requiring different things from us, existing on social media, and being fabulous lions, we can easily get caught up in the exciting parts of life and forget about things like food, hygiene, and general self-care. Physical, emotional, mental, and even spiritual burnout is a very real thing for the Leo witch.

A Leo forgetting to practice self-care is like a cat forgetting to groom themselves—such a combination shouldn't exist, but it does. Stress, depression, anxiety, and all sorts of other issues can make this simple task feel daunting. Leo portrays confidence because we want the people around us to be confident in us, but we actually need a lot of reassurance, which is why we can seem so outgoing. Having supportive relationships and feeling safe and secure at home are of the most importance to many Leos. We need to feel secure in these areas so we can go out into the world and do all of our Leo things!

Here are some simple and effective ways to recharge, de-stress, and groom your inner lion. All or some of these techniques can be combined to create an elaborate self-care ritual. Sometimes when we are feeling drained, it takes an entire day of luxuriating to get back to ourselves, and there is nothing wrong with that!

Moving Energy

Yoga, breath work, and meditation are all beneficial practices that have been especially helpful for me. These and other energy techniques like tai chi or qigong help focus and move energy so there is not buildup or stagnancy. It helps promote a sense of calm, rest, and rejuvenation. I personally prefer yoga and breath work because there is more physical movement. These practices can move excess energy to relieve stress and anxiety, as well as replenish depleted energy.

One technique that has been really helpful for me when it comes to grounding, remembering I have a physical body, and relaxation is taking a slow deep breath in, and then humming, vibrating, or singing on the exhale. This relaxed breathing combined with the different vibrations that can be achieved in your throat and torso has noticeable effects when a state change is needed.

Food for the Heart

Heart health is important for everyone, especially the Leo witch, who is ruled by the heart. Incorporating foods and herbs that support heart health are a simple way to practice self-love, heal the heart, and open it so that more love can flow through it.

 Rose (*Rosa* spp.) is one of my all-time favorite plant allies. It has a number of health benefits for the physical and subtle heart center. I like to add powdered rose petals to my protein shakes and take baths infused with rose. Rose is also a great herb for beautification and healthy skin and hair, which is why it can be found in so many cosmetics.

◊ Hawthorn (*Crataegus* spp.) is also a member of the Rosaceae family and is a powerful heart medicine. It is an amazing heart tonic that strengthens and supports. Powdered hawthorn berries or an extract of the berries is how I typically work with this plant. While it is an awesome dietary supplement, it also helps strengthen and protect the spiritual heart, helping us find courage and confidence.

◊ *Cacao* (*Theobroma cacao*) literally translates to "food of the gods." It is from the seeds of this plant that we make chocolate, and cacao has had a ceremonial significance throughout Central and South America. Cacao powder can be taken as a supplement, added to coffee, or brewed in warm coconut or oat milk. It is warming, uplifting, relaxing, and euphoric. The beverage opens the heart center, filling it with warm healing energy. It has also been used for its aphrodisiac properties, which is why it is perfect in ceremonies for reconnecting to your heart.

Preventing Social Media Burnout

These tips are especially important to people who spend a lot of time on social media for their livelihood but can also help anyone set up some good boundaries when it comes to conducting yourself on social platforms.

 Shungite is a popular stone that is used to prevent electromagnetic fields, Wi-Fi, and other electrical currents from interfering with our energy system. Prolonged exposure to cell phones, Wi-Fi, and even electrical wires can cause anxiety, stress, and other issues. Wearing a piece of shungite jewelry or keeping a stone next to you while you work helps keep you from getting sucked in and affected by exposure.

 Limit the amount of time you spend on social media or take at least one day a week where you completely disconnect. This may cause some anxiety at first, but that is a good thing. Once you get comfortable, you may want to increase to two days off! If you are a content creator, you have to take time off to create new content anyway. This means no messenger, no notifications, and no scrolling! By giving yourself some time away to recharge, you can come back with new ideas, and people will respect you for stepping away for yourself.

♦ Practice shielding exercises before getting online, and do cleansings afterward or on the days you take off. There is a lot of toxic energy floating around the ethers of the internet, and it is easy for something nasty to get attached to you. This is another reason why it is important to have strong boundaries when it comes to allowing social media into your day. It is easy for those energies to leak into your real life. Performing these exercises before and after engaging on social media tells the spirit world that *what happens in Vegas stays in Vegas!* This may not always be possible because we are off and on social media all day, but at least getting into the habit of consciously acknowledging the boundary and cleansing when you can is better than nothing.

♦ People naturally gravitate toward the Leo witch for help, and there are many individuals online who are looking for something. Our empathetic nature can make it easy for us to get caught up in online relationships because "people need us." Most people just need someone to talk to, and it is okay to be that person sometimes, but we can't let it interfere with our work or personal life. We can have strong boundaries and still be empathetic and be there for other people, but it has to be on our terms.

🔥 Don't sleep with your phone! Ideally keep your phone in a separate room when you are sleeping, unless you need it for your alarm. This is a really simple and powerful thing that can make a huge difference. Part of burnout comes from feeling like our personal space has been violated. By not allowing the technology into your sleep space, you claim that space for yourself.

🔥 Avoid arguing and engaging with trolls at all costs. It doesn't matter if you are right or not. It's like having to watch your parents fight at the dinner table. Don't do it!

🔥 Set up a personal profile where you can express yourself and only follow things that you enjoy. Limit your friends to people you connect with on a regular basis.

Opulent Rest

It can be hard work being a Leo witch, and it can be easy to forget to rest, because if we aren't creating, we're wasting time. You can enhance your rest and use your creativity by creating a resting space fit for royalty. This can be a separate space where you go to recharge throughout the day, or you can do this in your bedroom. This doesn't have to cost a lot of money; the key here is comfort and something aesthetically pleasing, so it is up to individual taste. Here are some suggestions that most Leo witches won't be able to resist.

 Rich colors (keep in mind this is a restful space)—deep reds, blues, violets, greens, gold, etc.

 Sheer fabrics over windows or lights, tapestries draped around bed/couch

 Different textures, materials, and patterns for sensory stimulation

 Fairy lights, electric candles, incense

 Pillows (you can never have too many pillows)

 Glamourous décor, anything shiny and opulent such as antique brass

 Tassels and beaded fabric

Anything that makes your resting space feel extra luxurious is an option, and the idea is to make your rest a royal event! I like to take a luxurious ritual bath before and wear nothing but a flowy robe or kimono afterward. When you awaken, rise to meet the world renewed!

Calendula Sun Bath

The yellow-orange flowers of *Calendula officinalis* or pot marigold look like tiny Suns. The bright flowers, when in bloom, seem to catch and reflect the sunlight. The herb has antifungal and antimicrobial properties, which protect and prevent infection. We can relate this to the light of the Sun removing stagnant energies. In addition to protecting the skin, calendula also helps heal the skin and improves its overall health and appearance! Calendula can be found in skin care products, made into infused oil, or added to bathwater for its rejuvenating and uplifting qualities.

We can make use of calendula's rejuvenating properties and the vitalizing energy of the Sun by making a solar infusion to add to a ritual bath. To make the infusion, add fresh or dried calendula flowers to a large mason jar or pitcher and fill it with water. Make sure it is covered so it doesn't get bugs in it but that it is still exposed to sunlight. Any sunny day will work, but you can also make it on Sunday to get an extra dose of solar energy. You can put the container out in the morning and collect it in the evening, and the water will be a golden yellow color. Strain this and add the liquid to your bathwater to infuse yourself with the Sun's healing energy, or pour it directly over yourself while you are sitting in the bath.

Sharpening Your Claws

Practicing good nail hygiene and/or getting regular manicures and pedicures is not only good for the health of your hands and feet, but it is also an easy way to practice self-care. I recommend everyone get a manicure and pedicure at least once in their lifetime. Having someone else touch your hands and feet isn't for everyone, but it can also be intensely relaxing! If you aren't interested in getting your nails done at a nail salon, you can find at-home nail kits in most stores that sell bath and beauty products.

Trimming and cleaning your nails is an activity that keeps our hands busy and allows us to focus our will on our intention. You can focus on removing built up energy and using your nails to tear through obstacles or imagine them turning into sharp adamantine claws capable of protecting against all enemies. You can enchant your nails to draw something you desire to you or to hold on to something you don't want to lose.

Nail shape, color, and designs make for infinite nail intention possibilities. This could be something subtle, like drawing runes on the nails in a clear coat with a nail art brush, or it could mean decorating them with green glitter and tiny strips of money to serve a look of abundance and prosperity! Our nails can show our personality, and because of their versatility, we can use them to communicate complex messages, thus making them the perfect vehicles for magickal intention.

At the end of every manicure, after the nail polish, the techs usually put on nail oil. This is my favorite part of a manicure because nail oil strengthens the nail plate and also moisturizes and heals the skin around the nails. Nail oil is what makes a manicure look flawless, and it can be used by itself to condition the nails. You can buy an actual nail oil at a beauty supply store, or you can use vitamin E oil. Here, you have the potential to create nail oils for specific intentions by adding corresponding herbs to the oil. Only add dry herbs when infusing oil. Apply this to the skin around the nails to nourish and moisturize.

* * *

All these techniques are things anyone can do, from breath work to personal hygiene and rest. By adding our intention and our Leonine perspective, we can create powerful daily rituals to keep ourselves strong, happy, and connected to the world around us based on our own unique needs. Every Leo has that something that makes them feel extra Lionlike; think Simba standing up on Pride Rock. Embrace those things that fulfill your inner lion, because when the Leo witch is happy and energized, the people around them become happy and energized!

Awakening the Three Lights and Invoking the God-Self

Gwendolyn Reece

As a Leo witch, light plays a key role in my magick, and I use a set of practices I consider "royal" because they are rooted in claiming your divine power. I believe we all will eventually evolve into gods (apotheosis). Once this transformation occurs, our God-Selves operate at a level unlimited by linear time that can be invoked. This technique is useful for spiritual development and empowering magick.

To begin, become aware of your blood—of the river of life that flows throughout your body—and of the interchange with your breath, infusing your blood with the power of pneuma. Place your mind into your blood. This is the seat of the ancestors. Everything they know and all their power is accessible here. Your blood is not mere substance—it contains life and light and knowledge. Fall through your blood until you find the light. Connect with that light and feel it flowing through your body. With conscious awareness, bring the light up and seat it at the top of your spine in the brainstem.

Now, become aware of your heart. Think of someone you truly love. Feel your heart opening and connecting. Feel the light of your soul reaching out in its purest and most powerful desire to comfort, to help, to connect. Let that light—the light of your personal soul—grow brighter, and brighter. Feel it grow so bright and large that it feels larger than your form can hold. Pull that light into your third eye behind your brow and see it shining. This is the first light.

Pull the light from and through your third eye—this is the second light—and have it join the light rising from your brainstem, entering the secret place in the center of your head about two inches below your crown. The third light resides in that central place. Feel the three lights in the center of your head, and then rise up, out through the crown of your skull—up until your center of consciousness is about one foot above your physical skull. Feel it fill with the light of your being. Draw the light up from your blood, your heart, from the middle of your head, into the place above your head, and feel it shine brighter and brighter like a beacon.

From this place, call to the god you will someday be—send out your light until you touch the Great Being who is outside of time and outside of space, but who is you. This Great Being stands outside of our current strife and never loses its center. If you know the name of your highest self, silently speak it. When you have made the conscious connection with your own God-Self, your Holy Guardian Angel, your Buddha Nature—however you know it—bring as much light and connection down with you into the center of consciousness above your skull. Then pull all the lights down into the secret place in the middle of your head. Know that you have grown deeper, brighter, and vaster.

DON'T BLAME IT ON YOUR SUN SIGN

Coby Michael

If you know the traits of your Sun sign, it can be easy to use them as an excuse when you display some of the more detrimental aspects of your sign, and we can also get stuck in a place where we can't escape our own bad behavior because we identify with it so much. In this section, we will look at some of the less-than-stellar qualities attributed to Leos, and how to avoid falling into their trap.

I think the important thing here is not to be too hard on ourselves. As Leos, this is especially true because we are always trying to live up to our own lofty expectations. Don't beat yourself up or feel doomed by what ultimately comes down to what other people think of you. Astrology is a very insightful and magickal tool, but it is not binding law. We don't have to feel like we are characters in a narrative of which we have no control; we are kings and queens and we make the rules!

Leo is often one of the most talked about signs when it comes to our less endearing qualities, right up there with Gemini and Scorpio. We have big personalities, so it makes sense that the other signs are paying attention to us! (Joking—sort of.) Some of the qualities stereotypical to Leo that people like to point out are that we are self-absorbed, vain, egocentric, arrogant, and lazy, to name a few. I can assure you, not one Leo I know has ever displayed one of these qualities. I certainly haven't.

Pride

This is the one that I have taken the most issue with. It is a good thing to be proud of who you are and what you put out in the world. Pride has always been a positive thing for me, from Gay Pride to my grandpa's pride at serving in the military. Pride can become a negative thing when we are too proud to ask for help because asking for help often involves admitting to someone that we can't do something by ourselves. Everyone needs support sometimes, and it doesn't diminish who you are as a person or what you've achieved to admit that you need help with something. When I think of pride in regard to being a Leo, it is usually a thing of arrogance, but I think it is about learning to be both proud and dignified. Taking pride in oneself doesn't mean we have to diminish others, and we shouldn't let feeling good about ourselves go to our head. It is important to remember where you started and remain humble no matter what you achieve.

Sense of Entitlement

You mean we don't get a trophy just for showing up and being a Leo? Leos are great at manifestation. We create sometimes without realizing it, and when you're used to things going a certain way, it can be difficult when they don't. I hate waiting rooms. I really loathe them because usually I'm waiting for something that I don't actually want to do, and I see all of the other people as obstacles to me doing whatever that thing is. If I can't get it done myself and other people aren't moving fast enough, I get very frustrated. So I often have to remind myself that I've planned plenty of time for whatever it is I'm doing and I'm not the only person in the universe with things to do.

Neediness

This could be emotional neediness or having physical things done. Leos need a lot of attention. We need reassurance that we are doing a good job, and that we are loved. We also love it when people feed us, clean up after us, and perform the list of tasks that we haven't had time to get to. It's a lot of work running a kingdom, and the more pressure we put on ourselves, the more pressure we put on the people around us. We have to remember that we are human and need to take care of ourselves sometimes so that other people don't have to! It's also super important to show gratitude for the people in our lives who are willing to put up with our nonsense. Like I've mentioned before, Leos are natural givers, but we usually have one or two people in our lives who we depend on the most who we could give a little bit more back to. Without them, the castle comes crashing down. We don't like to ask for help with the big stuff, but we have no problem asking for a million small things.

The following are some exercises that will help you embody your most regal Leo qualities and keep yourself in check on the others.

Gratitude Ritual

Make a list of three to five people who would be happy just to hear from you. This could be family, friends, or people you think need someone. Once you have their names down, write down one positive quality about them and one that they would describe you having. Thank them nonverbally for their friendship and their kindness, and then reach out to them. This can be a phone call, a message, or surprise someone with a classic handwritten letter! Just say hi and see how they are doing, and you will be surprised how great you both will feel afterward! Maybe even thank them for their friendship or for just being themselves. When someone is having a bad day, having a friend reach out can make all the difference. This ritual helps us remember the value of our relationships and the value that we bring to them.

Lion's Breath Mirror Affirmations

This technique comes from Indian yogic practices and is known as *simhasana* or *lion's breath*. It is a type of *pranayama*, or specialized yogic breathing that has a number of benefits from lowering stress to elevating mood. This can be done in a number of different sitting poses, including half lotus and cross-legged. The lion's breath technique has been said to lower blood pressure, increase cognitive function, and even lessen cigarette cravings!

Energetically, this technique focuses on stimulating the throat chakra, the energy center located at our physical throat responsible for communication and self-expression. When this chakra is operating properly, our messages come across clear and concise, and we communicate clearly and confidently. We are more in touch with our own truth and our ability to express that when the throat chakra is healthy.

You will need:

- A comfortable place to sit
- A mirror
- One or more affirmations to repeat

To perform the lion's breath, open your mouth wide, stick your tongue out to your chin, and make a *haaaa* sound with your breath. The lion's breath technique is said to relieve stress, eliminate toxins, and stimulate your throat and chest. It may feel silly at first, but it is a really effective technique to release emotions. It also can help with self-consciousness, speaking up for yourself, and having more confidence.

To intensify the technique and connect with the third eye, the gaze is focused upward on the middle of the forehead. I like to say a chant or mantra in my head before each breath—something encouraging like, "I embody strength and power," and then let out your roar. You can even use this practice to remove unwanted thoughts and emotions, and to stand your ground in certain situations by focusing on your intention. Simhasana can be performed at the beginning or end of meditation practice, or on its own throughout the day.

POSTCARD FROM A LEO WITCH

Aly Kravetz

When I step back and take a snapshot of my practice as a Leo witch, I see that my Sun sign shows up in my practice in some interesting ways. One of the most obvious ways is in my intense attraction to all things fire. I mean, if we're not lighting something on fire, are we even practicing magick? Personally, I think not. But on a much deeper and more serious level, I feel that being a Leo shows up in my desire and ability to work magick in the first place. Now, clearly I am incredibly biased here, and this is not to say that other zodiac signs aren't also magickly inclined, but I believe that the Leo spirit makes me exceptionally well equipped to practice magick because it is in the very nature of the Leo to do so.

As a Leo, I believe that I came to this Earth specifically to work magick. "I will" is the motto for the Leo zodiac sign. The Merriam-Webster dictionary defines <u>will</u> in a number of ways, but my favorite is "to express inevitability, persistence, insistence, or determination." To will something is to have both a laser-focused desire as well as the inability to accept anything other than the realization of this desire. It is an unwillingness to take no for an answer. And this unwillingness to take no for an answer provides the right container for effective magick. Aleister Crowley defines <u>magick</u> as "the science and art of causing change to occur in conformity with will." To me and many other practitioners, willpower is the driving force behind working magick. And Leos got willpower by the boatloads.

I will be honest and share that I did not always recognize this innate willpower as a good thing that supported and strengthened my practice. In fact, for many years, I was made to feel that my strong will was a bad thing. I grew up hearing phrases like hard-headed, stubborn, disagreeable, and headstrong and being told that these traits were unappealing and needed to be tamed. I believed this nonsense for a long time. I was so convinced that there was something wrong with expressing my will that for years I wouldn't say "as I will, so mote it be" at the end of my prayers or spells. I felt completely uncomfortable saying the words as I will. And my spells and magickal workings suffered for it. Thanks to time spent working on my inner child wounds with my therapist and soul-searching exercises like meditating with the Strength tarot card, I grew to realize that willpower is the gift given to Leo to help us navigate this crazy world.

These days, my will is first and foremost in my magickal practice and is the starting and ending point for all my magickal workings. I recognize that being hardheaded and strong-willed translates into effective and powerful magick, and so I make sure to tap into that part of myself through regular meditation and magickal practice. I also channel Leo energy into my workings as best as I can by doing things like working with the fire element or timing my spell work when the Sun, Moon, or particular planets are in Leo. The Leo witch uses willpower to turn desire into reality, and Leo energy shows up in our practice anytime we tap into our ability to will something into being.

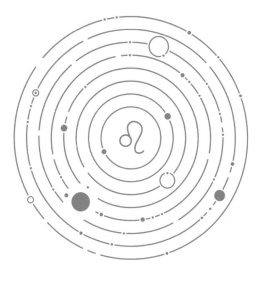

SPIRIT OF LEO GUIDANCE RITUAL

Ivo Dominguez, Jr.

The signs are more than useful constructs in astrology or categories for describing temperaments, they are also powerful and complicated spiritual entities. So, what is meant when we say that a sign is a spirit? I often describe the signs of the zodiac as the twelve forms of human wisdom and folly. The signs are twelve styles of human consciousness, which also means the signs are well-developed group minds and egregores. Think on the myriad of people over thousands of years who have poured energy into the constructs of the signs through intentional visualization and study. Moreover, the lived experience of each person as one of the signs is deposited into the group minds and egregores of their sign; they are ensouled. Every Leo who has ever lived or is living contributes to the spirit of Leo.

The signs have a composite nature that allows them to exist in many forms on multiple planes of reality at once. In addition to the human contribution to their existence, the spirits of the signs are made from inputs from all living beings in our world whether they are made of dense matter or spiritual substances. These vast and ancient thoughtforms that became group minds and then egregores are also vessels that can be used by divine beings to communicate with humans. The spirits of the signs can manifest themselves as small as a sprite or larger than the Earth. The shape and the magnitude of the spirit of Leo emerging before you will depend on who you are and how and why you call upon them.

There are many good ways to be a witch and a multitude of well-developed approaches to performing rituals. The ritual described in this chapter may or may not match your accustomed style, but for your first attempt, I encourage you to try it as it is written. Once you've experienced it, you'll see which parts, if any, you wish to adjust to be a better fit for you. I'll give some suggestions on how to do so at the end of this chapter.

Purpose and Use

This ritual will make it possible to commune with the spirit of Leo. The form the spirit will take will be different each time you perform the ritual. What appears will be determined by what you are looking for and your state of mind and soul. The process of preparing yourself for the ritual will do you good as well. Aligning yourself with the source and core of your energy is a useful practice in and of itself. Exploring your circumstances, motivations, and intentions is a valuable experience whether or not you are performing this ritual.

If you have a practical problem that you are trying to solve or an obstacle that must be overcome, the spirit of Leo may have useful advice. If you are trying to better understand who you are and what you are striving to accomplish, then the spirit of Leo can be your mentor. Should you have a need to recharge yourself or flush out stale energy, you can use this ritual to reconnect with a strong clear current of power that is compatible with your core. This energy can be used for magickal empowerment, physical vitality, or healing, or redirected for spell work. If you are charging objects or magickal implements with Leo energy, this ritual can be used for this purpose as well.

Timing for the Ritual

The prevailing astrological conditions have an impact on how you experience a ritual, the type and amount of power available, and the outcomes of the work. If you decide you want to go deeper in your studies of astrology, you'll find many simple or elaborate techniques to either pick the best day and time or to adjust your ritual to work with what fits your schedule. Thankfully, the ritual to meet the spirit of your sign does not require exact timing or perfect astrological conditions. This ritual depends on your inner connection to your Sun sign, so it is not as reliant on the external celestial conditions as some other rituals. Each of us has worlds within ourselves, which include inner landscapes and inner skies. Your birth chart, and the sky that it depicts, burns brightest within you. Although not required, you can improve the effectiveness of this ritual if you use any of the following simple guidelines for favorable times:

+ When the Moon or the Sun is in Leo, especially in the 15th degree of Leo.

- On Sunday, the day of the Sun, and even better at dawn.
- When the Sun is in Aries, where it is exalted.

Materials and Setup

The following is a description of the physical objects that will make it easier to perform this ritual. Don't worry if you don't have all of them; in a pinch, you need no props. However, the physical objects will help anchor the energy and your mental focus.

You will need:

- A printout of your birth chart
- A table to serve as an altar
- A chair if you want to sit during the ritual
- A candle—ideally a golden one, but any color will do (for fire safety, it should be in glass and on a plate or tray)
- An assortment of items for the altar that correspond to Leo or the Sun (for example, a sunstone, corn or cornmeal, and yellow flowers)

✦ A pad and a pen or chalk and a small blackboard, or something else you can use to draw a glyph

Before beginning the ritual, you may wish to copy the ritual invocations onto paper or bookmark this chapter and bring the book into the ritual. I find that the process of writing out the invocation, whether handwritten or typed, helps forge a better connection with the words and their meaning. If possible, put the altar table in the center of your space, and if not, then as close to due east as you can manage. Light the candle and place it on the altar and hold your hand over it. Send sparks of energy from your hand to the candle. Put the printout of your birth chart on the altar to one side of the candle and arrange the items you have selected to anchor the Leo and Sun energy around them. To the other side of the candle, place the pad and pen. Make sure you turn off your phone, close the door, close the curtains, or do whatever else is needed to prevent distractions.

Ritual to Meet the Spirit of Your Sign

You may stand or be seated; whichever is the most comfortable for you. Begin by focusing on your breathing. When you pay attention to the process of breathing, you become more aware of your body, the flow of your life energy, and the balance between conscious and unconscious actions. After you have done so for about a minute, it is time to shift into fourfold breathing. This consists of four phases: inhaling, lungs full, exhaling, and lungs empty. You count to keep time so that each of the four phases is of equal duration. Try a count of four or five in your first efforts. Depending on your lungs and how fast you count, you will need to adjust the number higher or lower. When you hold your breath, hold it with your belly muscles, not your throat. When you hold your breath in fourfold breathing, your throat should feel relaxed. Be gentle and careful with yourself if you have asthma, high blood pressure, are late in pregnancy, or have any other condition that may have an impact on your breathing and blood pressure. In general, if there are difficulties, they arise during the lungs' full or empty phases because of holding them by clenching the throat or compressing the lungs. The empty and the full lungs should be held by the position of the diaphragm, and the air passages left open. After one to three minutes of fourfold breathing, you can return to your normal breathing pattern.

Now close your eyes and move your center of consciousness down into the middle of your chest. Proceed with grounding and centering, dropping and opening, shifting into the alpha state, or whatever practice you use to reach the state of mind that supports ritual work. Then gaze deeply inside yourself and see a fire. The flames can be in a hearth, a bonfire, on a torch, or whatever feels right to you. Look at the dancing flames, hear the crackling, and feel the warmth. Reach out from that central fire and awaken all the places and spaces within you that are of Leo. When you feel ready, open your eyes.

Zodiac Casting

If you are seated, stand if you are able and face the east. Slowly read this invocation aloud, putting some energy into your words. As you read, slowly turn counterclockwise so that you come full circle when you reach the last line. Another option is to hold your hand over your head and trace the counterclockwise circle of the zodiac with your finger.

I call forth the twelve to join me in this rite.
I call forth Aries and the power of courage.
I call forth Taurus and the power of stability.
I call forth Gemini and the power of versatility.
I call forth Cancer and the power of protection.
I call forth Leo and the power of the will.
I call forth Virgo and the power of discernment.
I call forth Libra and the power of harmony.
I call forth Scorpio and the power of renewal.
I call forth Sagittarius and the power of vision.
I call forth Capricorn and the power of responsibility.
I call forth Aquarius and the power of innovation.
I call forth Pisces and the power of compassion.
The power of the twelve is here.
Blessed be!

Take a few deep breaths and shift your gaze to each of the items on the altar. Become aware of the changes in the atmosphere around you and the presence of the twelve signs.

Altar Work

Pick up the printout of your birth chart and look at your chart. Look at the candle on your altar. Touch each of the twelve houses with your finger and push energy into them. You are energizing and awakening your birth chart to act as a focal point of power on the altar. Put your chart back on the altar when it feels ready to you. Then take the pad and pen and write the glyph for Leo again and again. The glyphs can be different sizes, they can overlap; you can make any pattern with them you like so long as you pour energy into the ink as you write. Scribing the glyph is an action that helps draw the interest of the spirit of Leo. Periodically look at the items on the altar as you continue scribing the glyph. When you feel sensations in your body, such as electric tingles, warmth, shivers, or something that you associate with the approach of a spirit, it is time to move on to the next step. If these are new experiences for you, just follow your instincts. Put away the pen and paper and pick up the sheet with the invocation of Leo.

Invoking Leo

Before beginning to read this invocation, get in touch with your feelings. Think on what you hope to accomplish in this ritual and why it matters to you. Then speak these lines slowly and with conviction.

> *Leo, hear me, for I am born of the eternal fixed*
>   *fire.*
> *Leo, see me, for the Leo Sun shines upon me.*
> *Leo, know me as a member of your family and*
>   *your company.*
> *Leo, know me as your student and your protégé.*
> *Leo, know me as a conduit for your power.*
> *Leo, know me as a wielder of your magick.*
> *I am of you, and you are of me.*
> *I am of you, and you are of me.*
> *I am of you, and you are of me.*
> *Leo is here, within and without.*
> *Blessed be!*

Your Requests

Close your eyes and look within for several deep breaths, and silently or aloud welcome the spirit of Leo. Close your eyes and ask for any guidance that would be beneficial for you, and listen. It may take some time before anything comes through, so be patient. I find it valuable to receive guidance before making a request so that I can refine or modify intentions and outcomes. Consider the meaning of whatever impressions or guidance you received and reaffirm your intentions and desired outcomes for this ritual.

It is more effective to use multiple modes of communication to make your request. Speak silently or aloud the words that describe your need and how it could be solved. Visualize the same message but without the words and project the images on your mind's screen. Then put all your attention on your feelings and your bodily sensations that have been stirred up by contemplating your appeal to the spirit of Leo. Once again, wait and use all your physical and psychic senses to perceive what is given. At this point in the ritual, if there are objects to be charged, touch them or focus your gaze on them.

Offer Gratitude

You may be certain or uncertain about the success of the ritual or the time frame for the outcomes to become clear. Regardless of that, it is a good practice to offer thanks and gratitude to the spirit of Leo for being present. Also, thank yourself for doing your part of the work. The state of heart and mind that comes with thanks and gratitude makes it easier for the work to become manifest. Thanks and gratitude also act as a buffer against the unintended consequences that can be put into motion by rituals.

Release the Ritual

If you are seated, stand if you are able and face the east. Slowly turn clockwise until you come full circle while repeating the following or something similar.

> Return, return oh turning wheel to your
>   starry home.
> Farewell, farewell oh great-hearted Leo until
>   we speak again.

Another option while saying these words is to hold your hand over your head and trace a clockwise circle of the zodiac with your finger. When you are done, look at your chart on the altar and say,

It is done. It is done. It is done.

Afterward

I encourage you to write down your thoughts and observations of what you experienced in the ritual. Do this while it is still fresh in mind before the details begin to blur. The information will become more useful over time as you work more with the spirit of Leo. It will also let you evaluate the outcomes of your workings and improve your process in future workings. This note-taking or journaling will also help you dial in any changes or refinements to this ritual for future use. Contingent upon the guidance you received or the outcomes you desire, you may want to add reminders to your calendar.

More Options

These are some modifications to this ritual that you may wish to try:

+ Put together or purchase Leo incense to burn during the ritual. A Leo oil to anoint the candle is another possibility. I'm providing one of my oil recipes as an option.

+ Set up a richer and deeper altar. In addition to adding more objects that resonate to the energy of Leo or the Sun, consecrate each object before the ritual. You may also want to place an altar cloth on the table that brings to mind Leo, the Sun, or the element of fire.

+ Create a sigil to concentrate the essence of what you are working toward.

+ Consider adding chanting, free-form toning, or movement to raise energy for the altar work and/or for invoking Leo.

+ If you feel inspired, you can write your own invocations for calling the zodiac and/or invoking Leo. This is a great way to deepen your understanding of the signs and to personalize your ritual.

Rituals have greater personal meaning and effectiveness when you personalize them and make them your own.

LEO ANOINTING OIL RECIPE

* * *

Ivo Dominguez, Jr.

This oil is used for charging and consecrating candles, crystals, and other objects you use in your practice. This oil makes it easier for an object to be imbued with Leo energy. It also primes and tunes the objects so your will and power as a Leo witch flow more easily into them. Do not apply the oil to your skin unless you have done an allergy test first.

Ingredients:

- Carrier oil—1 ounce
- Frankincense—6 drops
- Orange—6 drops
- Rosemary—5 drops
- Cedar—4 drops
- Lavender—2 drops

Instructions:

Pour one ounce of a carrier oil into a small bottle or vial. The preferred carrier oils are almond oil or fractionated coconut oil. Other carrier oils can be used. If you use olive oil, the blend will have a shorter shelf life. Ideally, use essential oils, but fragrance oils can be used as substitutes. Add the drops of the essential oils into the carrier. Once they are all added, cap the bottle tightly, and shake the bottle several times. Hold the bottle in your hands, take a breath, and pour energy into the oil. Visualize light golden energy or repeat the word *Leo* or raise energy in your preferred manner. Continue doing so until the oil feels warm, seems to glow, or you sense it is charged.

Label the bottle and store the oil in a cool, dark place. Consider keeping a little bit of each previous batch of oil to add to the new batch. This helps build the strength and continuity of the energy and intentions you have placed in the oil. Over time, that link makes your oils more powerful.

BETTER EVERY DAY: THE WAY FORWARD

Coby Michael

Leos are creatures of fire. Fire is so innate to our entire being, our energy, and how we interact with the world. Fire can teach us a lot about ourselves, how to feed the flames, and what happens when they get too hot. Incorporating elemental fire into your magickal practice, you can gain a deeper sense for the fire burning within. What makes it burn brighter? How can you tend that fire to the best of your ability? This section explores the importance of sacred fire and how we can incorporate that into our Leo witch practice.

Keeping a ceremonial fire burning is an important ritual act in many cultures, one that goes back to time immemorial. By tending to our own inner flames, we can cultivate our energy and direct it in a specific way. We become more aware of our energy levels; this keeps our fire from burning too hot or too cold. If we allow other people and things to steal our fire, we are left with no energy. If we allow our emotions to get out of control, we can easily burn people nearby. The goal is to diligently tend this sacred fire, keeping it steady and bright. I have always felt very connected to the element of fire and regularly use it as a way to describe my energy. By using this metaphor, we can better connect with what is happening in our own energetic environment and how that is influencing others. There is a fire burning within each of us, a tiny Sun burning with passion.

Meditating with fire, visualizing it, and working with candles are powerful ways to connect with this elemental energy. We all have fire within us. It is the spark that ignites all life. Fire meditation can be a powerful tool for transformation, healing, and self-empowerment. We can tap into fire's transmutational properties and focus it toward our own personal growth. As fire signs, we have a natural affinity to the flame. As a visualization tool, fire can be a key to connecting with and directing your own personal energies. Fire breathing, spirit flames, and other visualization techniques can be incorporated into your energy work practice. Fire is cleansing, healing, and protective, and just as physical fire is honed in countless ways, inner fire may be harnessed for a variety of esoteric purposes.

I imagine this as a small Sun burning in the solar plexus, at the center of your being. When you are feeling inspired and connected to what you are doing, this Sun gives off a vital glow and seemingly endless energy. This is a feeling of warmth, contentment, and purpose. This fire can be a warning sign for things that are not aligned with our purpose, people or situations draining our energy, and things that we need to communicate so we can be at peace. When this fire ignites, we feel anxiety, anger, and a burning sensation in our solar plexus. This is often accompanied by a rush of adrenaline, pumping these intense emotions throughout the body. Once this fire starts burning, it easily consumes other things, and all of a sudden your entire life is ablaze!

Being aware of this inner fire and paying attention to how it changes is the first step to learning to work with it in a constructive way. It can tell us when a situation isn't working for us, and we need to express that to move forward. It can tell us when we have allowed our boundaries to be crossed and have developed unhealthy attachments to other people. Some people want to pour gasoline on our fire, and other people want to snuff it out. When we feel this feeling come up, it is important to release those feelings, and communicating how you feel can release a lot of the building pressure.

What is good fuel for your fire? There are some things that get our fires burning in uncontrollable and unhealthy ways, giving off toxic fumes. What are you intentionally fueling your fire with? What gives you purpose? What brings you joy? Who are the people in your life who make your fire burn brighter in a good way? Sometimes we can get carried away with our work or achieving a desired goal. We put so much into making that happen that we neglect to put fuel on our own fires. It is a great thing to work hard and passionately, but it is necessary that we give back to ourselves in order to continue giving to other people.

Burnout can lead to resentment and feelings of help-lessness. We can become frustrated with the people we care about when we feel like we have nothing left. Being ruled by the heart can sometimes mean not having the best boundaries. Boundary issues are oftentimes more prevalent with the people we love than with those we have no emotional connection with. Leos are known for being givers, but we have to remember to give back to ourselves too. When we overgive of ourselves, especially when we haven't been asked to, we can find ourselves feeling like our giving nature is not being reciprocated.

To start working on our boundaries, the firepit if you will, we must first be aware of where and what they are. We consciously and unconsciously agree upon the parameters of the boundaries of all our relationships and interactions. In order to please people or because of inner or outer pressure to live up to some expectation, we allow our boundaries to be compromised. This can leave us feeling violated, taken advantage of, or just overwhelmed.

You can use this visualization technique to detect where boundaries need to be reinforced. Sit in a comfortable position. I like to hold a fiery stone or crystal like carnelian, fire agate, or red jasper while I do this visualization, bringing the energies of fire and earth together for their protective power. I begin by doing breath work to get into a relaxed state of mind, feeling the warmth coming from the stone and connecting with the warmth of my solar plexus. As you inhale, imagine a transparent ball of fiery light coming from the center of your chest. As you draw in breath, the fireball grows larger, expanding to just outside of your physical body, containing you in a sphere of fire. When you exhale, the ball becomes smaller and more concentrated as you breathe into it. The ball becomes more concentrated with each inhale and exhale, and finally it is allowed to stretch out like a shock wave around you.

As the ball expands infinitely, it passes over all the people and things in your life. Most of the people it passes right over, but some of them cause the fire to be darkened or blocked. You can feel these blockages, like spots on the Sun. You may be able to see the people or things that are causing this, and maybe not. Exhaling, you draw your energy back into the center, concentrating it more than ever before. When it reaches its peak, you inhale and forcefully send the fire out again. This time, the attachments, not the people, are incinerated. Each time the ball of fire is expanded, more of these dark spots are illuminated, and every time the energy is brought back, your own personal boundaries are strengthened.

This is a powerful visualization, and it's not meant to hurt the people or things we are attached to, but to send a very strong message about our boundaries and how we keep our fire! Remember, one candle can light a thousand others without diminishing its own flame, and we can do the same for others.

Sometimes we are guilty of diminishing our own flames by scattering our energy in too many different directions, overworking ourselves and neglecting the health of our bodies. We also need to feed our fire and our bodies with physical fuel. Our fiery energy causes us to burn through our resources quickly, and it can be easy to forget things like food when you are working on a passionate project. Cooling, calming, and nourishing herbs and food are a good way to balance our fire and nourish our bodies. Cucumber, melon, rose, lemon balm, and lavender are all great places to start if you are an overheated fire sign. Home-cooked meals and nostalgic foods that feed your body and your heart are also a great way to connect with the ones you love and ground yourself in what is important. In the end, it is all about nourishing your inner lion to keep your inner fire burning strong and bright.

Golden Radiance of the Lion

Fio Gede Parma

The lion is said to be king of the jungle. A group of lions is called a pride. The female lion in particular possesses the prowess and strength of a skilled hunter and provider. In Western astrology, Leo the Lion is often considered the shining and radiant artist, the leader, the one who craves to be the center of attention. What is often left unsaid, especially in popular culture astro-memes, is the deep desire of the Leo to facilitate that radiance in everyone else around them. The golden radiance of the lion is magickly infectious. This working draws out that magickal charisma and casts it around us in order to stimulate the creative spirit of lushness, self-love, and cosmic centeredness in ourselves and those we meet.

You might like to time this working for either sunrise or midday when the golden radiance of the Sun is at the zenith of the arc of the day. In the spirit of the Self, you will need nothing else for this rite. This is about you and your connection with the infinite. That's it, that's all.

Standing if possible, or seated or lying down if required, bring your attention to the Sun. With your eyes open, engage your awareness with the rhythm of your breath. When you inhale, imagine, feel, or perceive that the golden radiance of the Sun is pouring down through you like a cascade of pure and holy fire. At the crest of your inhalation, hold for three counts and concentrate the golden light within with your powers of imagination and feeling. When you exhale, relax, move a little, make sound that helps you drop into this process. Sighing, laughing, toning, humming, or singing could work. Then pause for three counts before you breathe in again. Continue this process until you can sense or imagine that golden solar power pressing up against the edges of you.

You are gathering and concentrating this powerful golden radiance. At this point, start to guide and direct that light out past your surface-physical skin and into your aura. The following chant may aid you in this process:

Golden fire of radiance
Light of solar star dance!
Powers of beauty, love, and presence
Move through my every thought and sense!

Chant over and over until you feel that the power is peaking and the solar radiance is rippling through your aura intensely! When it becomes clear to you that you are about to reach the climax of this working, take a deep breath in, hold it for as long as you can, and then when you exhale with sound and emotion, feel and trust that the golden radiance of the lion is sealed within and through you. You will now be able to move through the world with the strength, power, beauty, and pride of Leo. Remember that each of the signs is within us. So mote it be.

CONCLUSION

Ivo Dominguez, Jr.

no doubt, you are putting what you discovered in this book to use in your witchcraft. You may have a desire to learn more about how astrology and witchcraft fit together. One of the best ways to do this is to talk about it with other practitioners. Look for online discussions, and if there is a local metaphysical shop, check to see if they have classes or discussion groups. If you don't find what you need, consider creating a study group. Learning more about your own birth chart is also an excellent next step.

At some point, you may wish to call upon the services of an astrologer to give you a reading that is fine-tuned to your chart. There are services that provide not just charts but full chart readings that are generated by software. These are a decent tool and more economical than a professional astrologer, but they lack the finesse and intuition that only a person can offer. Nonetheless, they can be a good starting point. If you do decide to hire an astrologer to do your chart, shop around to find someone attuned to your spiritual needs. You may decide to learn enough astrology to read your own chart, and that will serve you for many reasons. However, most practitioners of a divinatory art will seek out another practitioner rather than read for themselves in important matters. It is hard to see some things when you are too attached to the outcomes.

If you find your interest in astrology and its effect on a person's relationship to witchcraft has been stimulated by this book, you may wish to read the other books in this series. Additionally, if you have other witches you work with, you'll find that knowing more about how they approach their craft will make your collective efforts more productive. Understanding them better will also help reduce conflicts or misunderstandings. The ending of this book is really the beginning of an adventure. Go for it.

LEO CORRESPONDENCES

July 23–August 22

Symbol: ♌

Solar System: Sun

Seasons: Summer

Day: Sunday

Time of Day: Noon

Celebration: Spring Equinox

Runes: As, Rad, Wyn

Element: Fire

Colors: Gold, Green, Orange, Red, Scarlet, Yellow

Energy: Yang

Chakras: Solar Plexus, Heart

Number: 1, 4, 5, 8

Tarot: Strength, Sun, Wands

Trees: Acacia, Hazel, Holly, Juniper, Laurel, Oak,
Olive, Palm, Walnut

Herb and Garden: Angelica, Borage, Chamomile, Daffodil, Dill, Goldenseal, Heliotrope, Honeysuckle, Lavender, Marigold, Peony, Raspberry, Rosemary, Rue, St. John's Wort, Sunflower

Miscellaneous Plants: Anise, Cinnamon, Clove, Eyebright, Frankincense, Mistletoe, Nutmeg, Saffron, Sandalwood

Gemstones and Minerals: Amber, Beryl (Golden), Carnelian, Chrysoberyl, Citrine, Danburite, Diamond, Garnet, Jasper, Kunzite, Labradorite, Larimar, Onyx, Peridot, Rhodochrosite, Ruby, Sapphire, Sardonyx, Sunstone, Tiger's Eye, Topaz, Zircon

Metals: Gold, Pyrite

Goddesses: Anat, Bast, Cybele, Devi, Diana, Durga, Freya, Hathor, Hera, Inanna, Ishtar, Juno, Nanna, Sekhmet

Gods: Amun, Helios, Mithras, Nergal, Ra, Vishnu

Angel: Michael

Animals: Deer (Doe), Lion

Birds: Eagle, Peacock

Mythical: Sphinx

Issues, Intentions, and Powers: Action, Affection, Ambition, Authority, Communication (Eloquent), Confidence, Courage, Creativity, Determination, Energy, Enlightenment, Enmity, Friendship, Generosity, Growth, Guardian, Guidance, Integrity, Jealousy, Leadership, Life (Zest), Light, Love, Loyalty, Magick (Animal, Sex), Passion, Pleasure, Power, Pride, Romance, Strength (Controlled), Warmth, Willpower

Excerpted with permission from *Llewellyn's Complete Book of Correspondences: A Comprehensive & Cross-Referenced Resource for Pagans & Wiccans* © 2013 by Sandra Kynes.

RESOURCES

Online

Astrodienst: Free birth charts and many resources.

+ https://www.astro.com/horoscope

Astrolabe: Free birth chart and software resources.

+ https://alabe.com

The Astrology Podcast: A weekly podcast hosted by professional astrologer Chris Brennan.

+ https://theastrologypodcast.com

Magazine

The world's most recognized astrology magazine (available in print and digital formats).

+ https://mountainastrologer.com

Books

+ *Practical Astrology for Witches and Pagans* by Ivo Dominguez, Jr.
+ *Parkers' Astrology: The Definitive Guide to Using Astrology in Every Aspect of Your Life* by Julia and Derek Parker

- *The Inner Sky: How to Make Wiser Choices for a More Fulfilling Life* by Steven Forrest
- *Predictive Astrology: Tools to Forecast Your Life and Create Your Brightest Future* by Bernadette Brady
- *Chart Interpretation Handbook: Guidelines for Understanding the Essentials of the Birth Chart* by Stephen Arroyo

We give thanks and appreciation to all our guest authors who contributed their own special Leo energy to this project.

Jaime Gironés

Jaime Gironés (Mexico City) has practiced Witchcraft since he was thirteen. He writes about spirituality, minority religions, paganism, and Witchcraft in Mexico and Latin America. He is the author of *Llewellyn's Little Book of the Day of the Dead* and has contributed to *The Wild Hunt* as an international columnist.

Dawn Aurora Hunt

Dawn Aurora Hunt, owner of Cucina Aurora Kitchen Witchery, is the author of *A Kitchen Witch's Guide to Love & Romance* and *Kitchen Witchcraft for Beginners*. Though not born under the sign of Leo, she combines knowledge of spiritual goals and magickal ingredients to create recipes for all Sun signs in this series. She is a Scorpio. Find her at www.CucinaAurora.com.

Aly Kravetz

Aly Kravetz, a.k.a. BronxWitch, is a tarot reader, a Reiki practitioner, and an owner of BronxWitch HeadQuarters— a spiritual bookstore and work-share space in the Bronx, New York. Aly has been on her magickal journey since she was twelve years old and can be reached at www.bronxwitch.com.

Sandra Kynes

Sandra Kynes (Midcoast Maine) is the author of seventeen books, including *Mixing Essential Oils for Magic*, *Magical Symbols and Alphabets*, *Crystal Magic*, *Plant Magic*, and *Sea Magic*. Excerpted content from her book, *Llewellyn's Complete Book of Correspondences*, has been used throughout this series, and she is a Scorpio. Find her at http://www.kynes.net.

Fio Gede Parma

Fio Gede Parma is a Balinese-Australian, queer, nonbinary, initiated witch, mentor, and author. They currently reside in Gadigal and Bidjigal Country with a human and feline friend. Their website is www.fiogedeparma.com.

Lady Rhea

Lady Rhea is an accomplished author and known as The Witch Queen of New York. She has served the magickal community as a High Priestess of the New York Wica Tradition since 1972. Lady Rhea cofounded The Minoan Sisterhood with Lady Miw. To Lady Rhea, the magickal community is family.

Gwendolyn Reece

Gwendolyn Reece is a high priestess in the Assembly of the Sacred Wheel, leading Theophania Temple in Washington, DC. She is devoted to the Hellenic deities, especially Apollon and Athena. She serves as President of the Sacred Space conference and is a national teacher for the Theosophical Society in America.

David Salisbury

David Salisbury is a queer activist, Thelemite, and Feri initiate based in the Washington, DC area. He teaches primarily about the intersection of advocacy and magick around the country. He is the author of several books on magick, including *Witchcraft Activism* and *The Deep Heart of Witchcraft*.

To Write to the Author

If you wish to contact the author or would like more information about this book, please write to the author in care of Llewellyn Worldwide Ltd. and we will forward your request. Both the author and the publisher appreciate hearing from you and learning of your enjoyment of this book and how it has helped you. Llewellyn Worldwide Ltd. cannot guarantee that every letter written to the author can be answered, but all will be forwarded. Please write to:

Ivo Dominguez, Jr.
Coby Michael
℅ Llewellyn Worldwide
2143 Wooddale Drive
Woodbury, MN 55125-2989

Please enclose a self-addressed stamped envelope for reply, or $1.00 to cover costs. If outside the U.S.A., enclose an international postal reply coupon.

Many of Llewellyn's authors have websites with additional information and resources. For more information, please visit our website at:

www.llewellyn.com